THE SECRET POWER OF AN
EXPERT

—— BOOK ONE ——
"SUCCESS - AN ART OR A SCIENCE?"

THE SECRET POWER OF AN
EXPERT

BOOK ONE
"SUCCESS - AN ART OR A SCIENCE?"

VAL A. SLASTNIKOV

authorHOUSE®

AuthorHouse™ LLC
1663 Liberty Drive
Bloomington, IN 47403
www.authorhouse.com
Phone: 1-800-839-8640

Published by AuthorHouse   01/16/2014

ISBN: 978-1-4918-5030-5 (sc)
ISBN: 978-1-4918-5029-9 (hc)
ISBN: 978-1-4918-5028-2 (e)

Library of Congress Control Number: 2014900505

Contents

About the Author

Why am I the right person to write this book?

Recently I started having a "Matrix Syndrome". I started feeling that I am "The One". Just like Neo from the famous movie, I started thinking that it is my destiny, my life's goal to save all Experts of this World, to make their lives better, or at least to show them the better way, the better "modus operandi".

And I've got reasons to believe that I can. Not only do I know a lot about experts from my own experience—not only because I recruited them for my clients since 1998, but also because for the last 10 years I've also been an expert in my field. At first as a Talent Consultant, and later as a Technology Sales and Business Solutions Consultant. I was blessed with a chance to provide help to a whole lot of experts, and their lives were changed for the better due to my interference and the service that I've provided for them and for my Clients. I am proud to admit that for the last 10 years I have been a Consultant myself. I've been in the shoes of many experts on numerous occasions, so I know firsthand how it feels to be one.

My main reason for this book is to change the public's perception about experts. And to change the experts' perception about themselves. This book is an attempt to stop all experts in their tracks, and to show them that their life could be much better, much easier, and much more fulfilling. This is my manifesto, my personal outreach to all Experts of the World out there, in my hope for all of us to stop struggling, to turn it around—and, finally to start living.

And this is how the idea of **The Secret Power of an Expert** was born.

Why do you think I care so much about Experts? Because to me this is personal! I feel the same way about Experts as Barak Obama feels about Social Insurance. I heard him speak during the Election campaign when he said that the reason he felt so strongly about Public Insurance was because his own mother died of cancer at the age of 53. And when he was spending time with her in the hospital, he tried to call a number of Insurance companies to get coverage for her, and they all turned him down. So he made up his mind at that point that if he were to become the President of the United States he would change it around and make sure that every U.S. citizen would have equal access to Public Insurance whenever they need it.

It's the same thing with me. I wrote this book for my Dad who was an expert in Civil Engineering. He died early, at the age of 30. I wrote it for my friend Vlad. He was an expert in Computer Programming. He died early, at the age of 43. I wrote it for all my clients. Finally, I wrote it for myself. They say "You can't carry three, but you can help a thousand." I tried to carry three—been there, done that. I was trying to help out experts one at a time. Finding a better job for Expert A, trying to help Expert B find his next Project. Helping out Expert C to position his company in a new market . . .

Not any more! I want to help thousands, millions now! Why? Because now I know better. Because now I see that life is too short! Because I know how hard you work. I know what price you've paid to get where you are. Now, in recognition of your achievements, I want to give credit where the credit is due. I want to help you, I honestly do. And I want to help you succeed. Because now I know how to help you.
And I will.

Introduction. Why I care about experts and how to succeed in life

This book is for experts and about experts—specialists in their field.

Question # 1. Why do I care about experts?

In the last 10+ years of my professional career I was able to help out a lot of experts, but I also saw a lot of them struggling. So I kept thinking about how I could help more experts become more successful. I've witnessed many of my friends and even relatives who I considered to be great experts trying and even die trying to figure out how to succeed, all in vain. So I knew it was very important, yet very difficult.

And I saw a lot of them give up. But I did not give up and I kept searching.

For two long years I've been trying to find the secret success formula, the secret power of an expert. Here's what came out.

I sincerely hope that this book can help all experts out there to become happier and more accomplished in their lives and careers.

Question # 2. How to succeed in life?

Everything that happens in life happens for a reason.

I wrote this book because I wanted to help you succeed—that's all.

You got this book somehow, so I guess you must have been looking for an answer to that question. Maybe you've even been looking for awhile, but you were not getting the right answer?

How do you know though that this particular book will help you become more successful than tons and tons of other books out there you may or may not have read or heard of before?

You don't know that for sure, do you? So, why did you even bother getting it, then? There must be a good reason for that, right?

Oh yeah, because you've heard somewhere that anyone can achieve higher level of success, as long as they really work hard and they try hard at something . . . And if you don't succeed the first time—then try, try again . . . Right? Isn't it what they told us at school? Isn't that what most people think?

Can you become very successful based on that assumption? Does it mean that just by reading more and more about success you will be increasing your chances of being successful? Is our level of earning really dependent on our level of learning?

Maybe the answer lies in some particular book that you need to find? A course that you need to study? A diploma or a certificate you need to obtain? Or, like most other authors lead us to believe, the answer lies within us?

Well, I guess it depends on what you think success is, and what success means to you.

Suppose you think that success means being rich. Donald Trump once said, *"Getting rich is easy. Staying rich is harder."* (Donald J. Trump, 2004)

But, if you think success means being rich, and your idea of becoming rich is winning a lottery or working harder than others at your current job—please don't be offended if I tell you that you've got it all wrong, and that you are looking for success in totally wrong places. And you will see why, as we move along. So, as I said earlier, I don't know all the answers. But what I do know is this.

In my humble opinion, being successful highly depends on your ability to recognize what can help you become more successful in life—and what can lead you away from success.

You see, there's a great number of people out there whose life mission and professional goal is to achieve their dreams through helping others. These are the motivational speakers, the personal coaches, the solution providers, the trainers and the teachers. These are the Tony Robbinses, the Oprahs, the Mother Teresas and the Bonos of this world. Bill Gates, Sam Walton, Donald Trump, Steve Jobs—all these people provide tremendous amount of help, deliver exceptional value to their respective markets. These are the people that really empower us and help us grow—spiritually, intellectually and professionally.

But there is a great number of people out there who are involved in manipulation of others. They are engaged in mass deception on a local, national or even on a global scale. Their business is very lucrative, but at the same time it is detrimental to those uninformed and misled people who, willingly or unwillingly get involved in their schemes. And the worst thing is that their victims are totally unaware of the amount of damage that mass deception is causing them and their families.

(Don't worry, Frank Kern—I'm not talking about you, my friend . . . ;-))

What if I told you that I could help you in your quest for success. What if I told you that I can help you recognize who's your friend and who is your worst enemy on that journey? Would it be a good reason for you to continue reading?

OK, you are probably thinking. So, what else is this book about?

This book is the first step in my long-term mission that I've started 10 years ago. As I told you earlier—my mission is to help you succeed. The mission of this book, however, is to caution you in your quest for success, to teach you how to recognize the right ways to approach success and how to set them apart from those ways that can potentially harm, even damage your life, your well being and your professional or business career. This book is intended to open your eyes and make you become conscious of life and business decisions you make in life.

Book One ~ An Art or a Science? ~

Goals of Book One

There are 3 major goals that I am trying to accomplish with this book:

Number One Goal is to prove to you that Success is a pure Science—and not an Art.

Number Two Goal is to show you what you need to know for your Success journey to be successful.

Number Three Goal is to show you exactly what you should be focusing on in the start-up stage of achieving prosperity as an Expert.

This book is a result of a tremendous effort. I started writing it at the beginning of 2007. I spent 5 years writing it and I have done a lot of research, a lot of leg work for you. All you need to do is read this and try to understand as much as you can, and then decide who your friends and who your enemies are. And after that—and only after that!—you can start developing or adjusting your own success strategy.

However, before I send you on a Journey to Success, let me finish this introduction with a quotation from Leo Burnett, one of the biggest advertising giants of the last century who said, *"When you reach for the stars you may not quite get one, but you won't come up with a handful of mud either."* (Burnett)

It will be my pleasure to help you along the way. Let me be your trusted advisor, your faithful yeoman, your humble servant with a caring heart . . .

The Future is Bright. Keep Smiling!

Val Slastnikov

Chapter 1. Wake Up Call

So, you say you're an expert . . . but is it enough?

MY BOOK IS A WAKE-UP CALL FOR EVERYONE WHO CONSIDERS HIMSELF OR HERSELF TO BE AN EXPERT.

No matter if you are running a highly specialized company (IT Consulting firm, for example), or you have a successful fashion/modeling/recruiting or any other kind of agency that specializes in a particular market, or you may just consider yourself to be an expert in something, like rocket science or catching flies—this book is for you.

This book is not for generalists—it is for specialists. It is for those who already became experts and for those who are striving to gain an expert status some day.

Regardless of where in the world you are located right now—I don't care if you're in the middle of Sahara Desert or at the bottom of Atlantic Ocean—if you think that you are a specialist in whatever you do—this book is for you!

Do you know what the best definition of 'an expert' is? According to Tim Knox, "It's someone who knows just a little bit more than the next guy." (Knox)

Why is it a wake-up call? Because the Experts of this world tend to believe that being an expert, i.e. "knowing just a little bit more than the next guy" is all they need to be successful! And I'm here to tell you that it's simply not true. The truth is—if you believe that your education, your experience and the fact that you specialize is all that you need to create a flood of contract offers rushing to your door—you are fooling yourself.

And YOU will be the one paying the price of these self-defeating beliefs. Not someone else—YOU. Trust me—I've been there myself. These beliefs are nothing but the road to everlasting struggle, to everlasting pain, loneliness and, ultimately, complete failure and even self-destruction.

Listen, you need to do much better than just BE an expert. You have to PROVE it to people. And you have to prove it to them on a massive scale.

This is the book that will show you how to do it. This is the book that will show you the way to success. This is the book that will show you the way to freedom. This is the book that will change your mind.

You will want to share what you've learned with all your relatives and friends, and you will want to change the way you do things right now. Why? Because you will know you should, before it gets too late!

This book is needed now more than ever, and here's why.

Rich Schefren, who is a highly acclaimed online guru coach and a great online marketer, has recently said in one of his coaching videos that *"the battle for the consumer becomes more and more fierce these days. More companies are being created every day— online and offline. We are overloaded with information, and people are desperately searching for experts to help them deal with that information overload, to help them make the right choices. Customers are seeking for experts because they don't know where to go, what to buy and simply who to trust."* (Schefren, Strategic Profits Vault)

Why? Because there are too many choices, and your clients are tired, scared and confused. That's why they need experts to help them decide what to do.

THEY NEED YOU. THEY WANT YOU TO DECIDE FOR THEM.

But are they finding you—did you ever think about that?

Tell me, how are they supposed to find experts if the overwhelming majority of them are working with one client at a time. Huh?! Yes, some experts handle several projects at a time, but the majority of experts work on one project, with one client at a time.

And do you know what the experts do with the rest of their time?

. . . They are looking for a new project!

They are very smart people, those experts. I am sure they realize how important it is to promote themselves. But the reality is that they simply have no time for that. Or, they have no idea how to do it. Or, they are used to doing it the hard way, like many talented people before them.

So, instead of promoting themselves, instead of proving how good they are on a massive scale, instead of positioning themselves as experts in their respective fields, markets and niches—they spend all their time working—or looking for work!

. . . What a waste of talent and opportunity!

I'm a big fan of rock music, especially of the 70's when the big bands like Pink Floyd and Dire Straits gave the world such iconic expressions as *"Hanging on in quiet desperation is the English Way"* (Floyd, 1973) and *"The game commences for the usual fee, plus expenses"* (Knopfler, 1982)

But that was the 'Good Olde' 70's, and unfortunately a lot of us Experts are still living our lives, as if we are stuck in the time warp. No wonder that the younger generation, with their iPods and YouTube, is passing us by—isn't it because we are totally oblivious to what's going on around us? Isn't it time for us to start learning from the 'kids of today'? Isn't it time for us to stop *"hanging on in quiet desperation"*? Isn't it time for us to stop trading our skills *"for the usual fee, plus expenses"*?!

So, this book is my personal quest, my intimate journey, the way to discover Freedom for My Generation.

This is a book about revelations, the "a-ha" moments, the life-changing information. This is a book that has a new approach to marketing yourself as an Expert, and to promoting yourself as an Expert. And, most importantly, it's about maintaining that 'obvious expert' status in the mind of your clients—for years and years to come.

This is a book about prosperity—your prosperity AS AN EXPERT!

Chapter 2. Definitions of Success and Failure

"The single most important principle in the field of interpersonal relations is this: Seek first to understand, then to be understood. Most people listen, not with the intent to understand, but with the intent to reply."

\- Steven R. Covey (Covey, 1991)

Here's some compelling reasons for you to stop, focus and analyze your current situation. And then start changing it. Slowly. Carefully. One step at a time.

But . . .

In order for us to make daily progress in our journey to success, let's make it a rule:

First—we define.

Then—we analyze.

And only after that—we decide whether we can apply it or not. Agreed? Let us commence our Journey to Success then!

I am sure that you understand that Success is a journey—not an event. But what does the word 'Success' mean?

According to Wikipedia:

*"**Success** may mean:*

- *a level of social status*
- *achievement of an objective/goal*
- *the opposite of failure"* (Wikipedia, Success, 2010)

According to this definition, success may mean many things. (The key word is 'may' here). Success happens when you advance in social rankings, it happens when you achieve your dreams, goals, aspirations, etc. Success is NOT failure, it's quite the **opposite** of that.

So, in order for us to understand what leads to success, first let's try to get a better idea of what leads us to failure, which is quite opposite of success.

Again, according to Wikipedia:

*"In general, **failure** refers to the state or condition of not meeting a desirable or intended objective. It may be viewed as the opposite of success."* (Wikipedia, Failure, 2010)

Why do people fail? Huh?!

I am convinced that most people fail because of the way they think about success and the way they think about achieving success. Time and time again, I see the following pattern.

According to Ken Evoy, an Internet pioneer, there are these 10 types of mentality that lead to failure or a complete disaster: (Evoy, 2004)

1. The Blame Caster Mentality

That is someone who tends to blame everyone and everything around them—but not himself or herself. And if it ever is their fault, their best defense is a good offense—they just go ballistic!

2. The Angry Ones

The worst case of Blame Caster Mentality. These people make everyone feel miserable. These are the ones that blow up at anything and anyone and blame everyone for everything, except themselves. People run from them because they are constantly in fights. They spend a lot of time flaming in forums, and fighting with support staff all around the globe. These are the tough ones to change. My best advice to you is this:
'Stay as far away from them as possible!'

3. The Cynic Mentality

The one who trusts no one—not even himself/herself! This person simply believes everyone does something for a covert, manipulative reason. It's a sad life to lead . . .

4. Get Rich Quick Mentality

These people actually believe that companies would SELL 'Get-Rich-Quick' Formulas . . . that work! Their idea of becoming rich is winning a lottery, inheriting money from their relatives after they die or marrying a Prince . . . or a Princess. They think that there IS free money hidden out there—just for them to take! As long as THEY don't have to do any work, that is . . .

5. The Entitlement Mentality

An evolved version or variation of 'Get Rick Quick' type. These people believe that the world owes them a living. Widely perceived as whiners, they expect others do everything for them. Usually THOSE are the ones that expect everything for free . . . And not only for free, but NOW! These are the ones that applaud socialism, look for a Genie in a Bottle and end up on welfare—a place where they really belong!

6. The Envious Ones

These people are jealous of others' success. They count other people's money before their own. They hope that the winners will fail . . . eventually. They can never be successful because they can only focus on what others seem to be doing—not their own success . . . These are the ones who believe that Success is an Art—and end up broke worshiping the Stars, as opposed to start building your own success in life.

7. The IQ-Challenged

These people just don't have the smarts to become successful in life. The fact of the matter is—they would be better off in doing some manual work.

Let's be realistic! Success is not for everyone. And if it was really THAT easy—everyone would be doing it, right?

8. The Liar/Cheater Mentality

For these folks, it's easier to lie and cheat than to do it honestly. These are the ones that sell you 'Get-Rich-Quick' schemes. Those are the ones who smile in your face, and stub you in the back. Those are the ones who believe that *"There's a sucker born every minute."* Rich Schefren said about those, *"You can make money lying, cheating, hustling, but you can't build a business that way. Why? Because business is a long term thing, and eventually you will be found out."* (Schefren, Strategic Profits Vault).

After all, as Abraham Lincoln said, *"You can fool some people all the time, you can fool all people some of the time, but you can't fool all people all the time!"* (Lincoln)

9. The Nitpicker Mentality

These people are 'Perfectionists'. They can miss a forest of success by spending too much time trimming the trees. These folks tend to focus on the wrong things and can't move ahead until everything is "Just Perfect". With a bit of coaching they can do extremely well though.

10. The Quitter

These are the ones that give up at the first obstacle. These are always looking for a project with no problems. They hate problems. They would rather quit than deal with them. These are the ones that complain a lot, too. Luckily, it's easy to recognize them, as they are the ones that disappear early in the game.

If you recognized yourself in one of those Mentality types—great! You have something to work on, and this is a great way to start changing your mind from being 'doomed to fail' to being "geared towards success" . . .

Chapter 3. Lottery Statistics

"Insanity: doing the same thing over and over again and expecting different results."

- Albert Einstein (Albert Einstein Quotes)

Have you ever won any significant amounts of money by playing lottery?

If yes—good for you! But the majority of people admit that they won very little, very seldom, or never won anything at all. In fact, someone asked that same question on Yahoo Answers not long time ago—and here's what the answers were (I quote):

"$5 from a scratch off that I was given for xmas" (Unknown, 2006)

"5 bucks."

"no, hopefully someday though"

"$10.00"

"25"

"most 20.00 NY lotto stinks"

"50 bucks . . . spent it all on losing tickets LOL"

"No-None- Zilch- Zedo-"

"5 lousy bucks. not worth the time. certainly not the investment . . ."

And, my favorite one:

"No I never have because I believe that playing the lottery is like a tax on the mathematically challenged."

I guess you'll agree that these answers definitely reflect what the majority of people experience when playing the lottery, right?

So, how come that the majority of us never experience *success through winning the lottery?*

Because there is such thing out there that is called Statistics. Statistics deals with numbers, and numbers don't lie. Statistics shows for example that, according to 'Winning a Lottery for Dummies':

"Most of us play a lottery with 49 different balls, and 6 balls get drawn.

So that means, it's 49 x 48 x 47 x 46 x 45 x 44 = 10,068,347,520.

That's a big number and an awful lot of combinations! But don't fret too much. Don't forget that it doesn't matter what order the balls are drawn!

Here's another time saver—as it would take forever to work out how many times combinations are repeated by writing them all down . . .

It's simply 6 x 5 x 4 x 3 x 2 x 1 = 720.

So what, then, are my chances of winning the lottery?

Well, you've pretty much worked it out. It's 10,068,347,520 divided by 720, which comes out at roughly 1 in 13,983,816." (Chances of Winning the Lottery - for Dummies ;-))

This means that the chances of becoming successful by winning a lottery is 14 million to 1!!!

And the odds of winning the Mega Millions Jackpot are even worse—it's said to be 1 in 175 Million!

. . . So, let me ask you this:

Why on Earth are you still playing???

As you saw from the above explanation, only a very small percentage of people ever win anything, no matter what type of lottery they play and no matter what the lottery companies are saying.

On the same note, your chances of marrying a Prince, or a Princess are limited by the number of living Princes and Princesses, which is, like 14 who might be eligible and not married already, compared to the total number of 4 billion people that live on this planet . . . Don't you see how ridiculously small your chances are?

Chapter 4. An Art or a Science?

"The road to recovery starts with recognition."

- Paul Lemberg, Business Strategist (Time Management Secrets: Getting More Done)

And if you think you'll succeed by working harder than others (because that's what your boss wants you to believe!) you've got another thing coming once again. Most certainly, you will get tired more as a result of working harder and longer hours, but in all honesty—you will never be able to become rich that way! Yes, your company and your boss will become richer—but not you!

The idea of a job security is also false. I don't know exactly who said it, but I think this is so true: "**Job security** is a **myth** perpetuated by employers to get and keep employees in subservience for their entire lives to the benefit of the employer in the end." Also, Benjamin Franklin once said that "the man who trades freedom for security does not deserve nor will he ever receive either." (Franklin, 2010)

Of course, you might get a Christmas bonus, or get promoted one step higher. But that is all that you will ever going to get, my friends!

Stop fooling yourself!

And if it sounds discouraging, I am sorry that I had to break it to you like that. Sorry that I had to disappoint you. You see, in order for me to help you, I have to be brutally honest with you. I have to tell you the truth. Because you've heard enough lies in your life already. And the real reason you bought this book was not to continue fooling yourself, but to discover the truth, am I correct?

So please understand—whatever you heard at school, at work, from your friends and relatives—those were all misconceptions! A little bit of hocus- pocus, a bunch of baloney, and a whole lot of smoke and mirrors, my friends!

Please understand one thing. That's **not** how wealth has been created in the past, that's **not** how it is being created today, and most certainly not how wealth will be created in the future . . .

If you think **success means being famous**, and your idea of becoming famous is creating a series of YouTube videos about how cute your cat is or how much you love Paris Hilton—I have to disappoint you—once again! That's not how people become famous either!

Here's what Derek Gehl, the President and CEO of Internet Marketing Center, a $100-million company has to say about that: " . . .*Creating a network of 500+ friends on Facebook and MySpace, or recording endless videos to post on YouTube, is a ridiculous waste of your time if you're not able to convert these friends and fans into customers.*" (Gehl, 2008)

. . .I totally agree with you, Derek on this. Unless, of course you guys submit your video to "America's Funniest", it wins a $100,000 prize and you become instantly famous . . . But even still, this is more of an exception—not the rule.

And it makes me smile when I see that some folks decide to become famous by getting on Speakers' Corner (the Toronto's popular TV program) and talking their heads off about how much their life sucks. No one will listen to you anyway . . . Why? Because everyone else's life sucks the same way, or even worse—that's why . . .

Alrighty then . . . I know what you're thinking . . . **there is a big success somewhere out there.** People do become rich and famous all the time . . . But what is it that they do differently that makes them successful? And how can you do the same things they do and **become successful, too?**

Well, here's what it boils down to . . . It all depends on what you believe in. Like, do you believe that **success is an Art** or do you believe that **success is a Science**?

I challenge you to give me an honest answer.

But . . .

You have to be careful here . . . Why? Because if you view success as an Art, you probably think that only talented people can be successful. And if you do not have any talent—you are doomed, and you will never become rich, famous, let alone both.

If you view success as an Art, you might as well close this book right this minute, get back to your favorite TV channel or to your boring job (that is, of course if you even HAVE a job, as some people are not even there yet, I swear to God!) . . .

In fact, I will even go further and make a statement that lots of you folks will probably disagree with:
If you think that success is an Art—then being successful is not for you!!!

Keep on reading stupid articles about celebrities and their successes, send them passionate messages on MySpace and Facebook and tell them how much you admire them, how wonderful and talented they are, and how boring and mediocre **your** life is, compared to theirs . . . Or, better still—don't even bother looking at celebrities. Just look at your friends, your parents and your relatives who never ever achieved any success in life, and say to yourself, "Well, if they never achieved anything, why should I even bother trying . . . ?" You can find consolation in a good old Nirvana song,

"I'm so ugly . . .

It's OK 'cos so are you . . . etc." (Cobain, 1991)

And, if you **do** find consolation in this, I strongly suggest that you take this book and return to wherever you bought it from, and ask for a full refund . . . I will make sure that they will give you your full money back, because I don't want you to waste your time any longer . . .

Did you get the idea yet? Why am I being so brutally honest and merciless with you here? Because I'm such a mean person?

No, I am not trying to offend you or belittle you whatsoever—that's not my intention, my friends.

I already told you that all I'm doing is trying to help you realize what is really going on out there.

What I am really alluding to is that **there is** an alternative thinking, an alternative belief out there. And if you believe **that success is a Science**—all of a sudden you start believing in yourself, too.

Why?

Because if you believe that **success is a Science,** you will believe me if I say that success can be studied, measured, engineered and created with the scientific precision. And, most importantly, unlike talent, success can be shared, taught and passed on to other people . . . Heck, even to other generations!

OK, now that you know this—let's move forward.

Chapter 5. Values are Forever

"A Diamond is Forever"

- De Beers Slogan (De Beers, 1947)

Now that you know that Success is something that can be created, you are starting to realize that you don't have to be in Hollywood to be successful, you don't have to be a Superstar—in fact, you don't need to be any kind of a Celebrity at all! Heck, you don't even have to be talented, or even smart, in order to be successful—I swear!

(If you don't believe me—keep reading, and I'll prove it to you later—I promise!)

So . . . what do you need to have instead of being talented then?

Well, what you need is to **listen, learn and do** things right.

What things?

I will tell you. Remember what we've talked about in the previous Chapter? I told you it's all about what you believe in, what kind of Values you have in life.

Wikipedia defines Value like this:

"Value is a concept that describes the beliefs of an individual or culture." (Wikipedia, Value, 2010)

A Value is something that we strongly believe in, and values usually do not change—like diamonds, they retain their constant power and importance in our lives. This is why I called this chapter "Values are Forever".

I know from my own experience that I very rarely change my own values, if at all. If I ever believe in something—I always believe in it. But you don't have to take my word for it. If you look at the List below, you can easily see what people **value the most** in their lives:

Common Values

Accomplishment	Flair	Progress
Success	Freedom	Prosperity
Accountability	Friendship	Wealth
Accuracy	Fun	Punctuality
Adventure	Global view	Quality of work
All for one and	Good will	Regularity
one for all	Goodness	Resourcefulness
Beauty	Gratitude	Respect for
Challenge	Hard work	Others
Change	Harmony	Responsiveness
Cleanliness	Honesty	Results-oriented
Collaboration	Honor	Rule of Law
Commitment	Independence	Safety
Communication	Inner peace	Satisfying
Community	Calmness	Others
Competence	Quietude	Security
Competition	Innovation	Self-giving
Concern for	Integrity	Self-reliance
others	Justice	Service
Content over	Knowledge	(to others,
Form	Leadership	society)
Continuous	Love	Simplicity
improvement	Romance	Skill
Cooperation	Loyalty	Speed
Coordination	Maximum	Spirit in life
Country, love of	Utilization	(using)
(Patriotism)	(of time,	Stability
Creativity	resources)	Standardization
Customer	Meaning	Status
satisfaction	Merit	Strength

© 2014 Val A. Slastnikov "The Secret Power of An Expert"
Book One "Success - An Art or a Science?"

Decisiveness	Money	Succeed; A will
Delight of being,	Orderliness	To
joy	openness	Achievement
Democracy	Peace, Non-	Systemization
Discipline	violence	Teamwork
Discovery	Perfection	Timeliness
Ease of Use	Personal	Tolerance
Efficiency	growth	Tradition
Equality	Pleasure	Tranquility
Excellence	Positive	Trust
Fairness	attitude	Truth
Faith	Power	Unity
Family	Practicality	Variety
Family Feeling	Preservation	Wisdom
	Privacy	
	Problem	
	Solving	

I learned from experience that the most valuable things are also the most scarce in life, it is something that we all do not have enough of!

What it means is that **we should be working the hardest at achieving things that we value the most.**

Let me illustrate this by using investment capital as an example of a scarce commodity.

We live during difficult times. We all know that investment capital is the fuel of our Economy, especially small businesses that are very fragile and most of the time they can't survive without significant infusions of the investment capital—especially when we talk about charitable and non-profit organizations. However, our bank system is going through crisis right now and can no longer provide investment capital to small business owners for growth or start-up of their businesses.

© 2014 Val A. Slastnikov   "The Secret Power of An Expert"
Book One "Success - An Art or a Science?"

The Financial Experts predicted the crisis many years ago and explained why capital does not like economic instability:

"Capital has three important characteristics. It is mobile, sensitive to its environment and scarce. Therefore capital is extremely selective. It attempts to settle in countries or localities where government is stable, economic activity is not over-regulated, the investment climate is hospitable and profitable investment opportunities exist." (CSI, 2008)

As we can see here, it gets more and more difficult for people to retain the values that we created. Even money requires special treatment and does not just come to anyone anywhere—you have to earn its trust and attention, in order for you to attract it, whether you believe it or not!

But enough about money for now. What about love, another scarce commodity that we value so high?

Think about this for a second.

If love is your highest priority then you have to make it your goal to attract love into your life, develop a plan on how to attract love and work on realizing that plan each and every day of your life until love finally comes to you. You have to be intentional and proactive in bringing it closer.

Sounds too generic, doesn't it?

OK, let's become more specific then.

What I suggest you should do as an exercise in attracting love is make a list of things that you feel grateful for, things that you already have in your life.

It can be somewhat like this:

I am grateful for my:

Children
Parents
Job
Health
Pets

Or:

I feel grateful for:

Being born in this country
Being able to get rid of my debt
The food on my table
The Partner that I have in my life
The Mentor that I was able to find for me
The Sun that is shining
The Birds that are singing . . .

Now, after you see what you already have—get back to the List of your Values and see if the things you value the most are already present in your life.

If you don't have enough of what you value the most—you have some work to do!

Let's say that you value friendship very highly, but you don't have many friends right now . . . Do you think you can change it?

Of course you can! You can become a member of a Social group, a club, you can meet new friends in the church, at work, at your doctor's office, at a party, etc.

That's OK—you'll say. Friendship is good, it's all fine and dandy, but how can I become more successful in life? What are my options?

A-ha! I'm glad you asked! The question like that is a first step on the way to systematic thinking. I have to stress that point, as it is highly important, my friends. If you've asked yourself that question, then there is an opportunity for me to help you, and that is what makes me feel very happy. So here's your answer . . .

Chapter 6. Systems Make All the Difference

Yes, my friend. The answer is very simple:

"You have to develop a system!"

The thing is, developing a system is very important because those who **have a plan, a system in their life** usually become successful. The opposite is also true: those who don't have a system of some sort in their lives almost always end up broke.

So, let's talk about systems a little bit, and try to understand why it is so important to have a system. We say "Educational system", "Government system", "System of Values" . . . But what does the word **'system'** mean anyway?

According to Wikipedia:

"System (from Latin systēma, in turn from Greek σύστημα systēma) is a set of interacting or interdependent entities, real or abstract, forming an integrated whole.

There are natural and man-made (designed) systems. Man-made systems normally have a certain purpose, objectives. They are "designed to work as a coherent entity". Natural systems may not have an apparent objective.

A system is a fundamental concept of systems theory, a way of thinking about the world, a model." (Wikipedia, System, 2010)

A-ha! So, as we find from here, there's a whole system of thinking out there, and it was developed for a reason . . . Someone took their time and made an effort to develop a whole Theory of Systems for us . . .

Why?

Well, maybe because they treated Success **as a Science,** and wanted to build a System that would make **them** successful, eh? What do you think? ;-)

Let's dive in deeper and take a little peak into what Systems Theory is . . .

Are you excited yet, folks? Well—I am! Check this out. More of Wikipedia for you:

"Systems theory is an interdisciplinary field of science and the study of the nature of complex systems in nature, society, and science. More specifically, it is a framework by which one can analyze and/or describe any group of objects that work in concert to produce some result." (Wikipedia, Systems theory, 2010)

In Summer of 2008 I took a course in Business Risk Management, where I learned that frameworks are very important for businesses, in order to minimize risks and to establish compliance with laws and regulations.

So, what is a **framework,** then?

Well, a framework is just a structure, a system that helps solve or address complex issues, like risk and compliance—that's all.

Do you see that Wikipedia says the same thing I told you at the beginning of this chapter: We can analyze and describe any group of objects that work in **concert,** that create a system and that produce some result—positive or negative—including Success!

OK. So, why do you need a system, you ask? Simple! Not to fail—that's why!

Because people fail 80% of the time and a system always wins.

You know what the acronym SYSTEM stands for?
Save **Y**our **S**elf **T**ime, **E**nergy and **M**oney!

If you're still wondering why on Earth you would need a system, let me tell you this:

Either you will have a System, or the System will have you!

Period.

Unfortunately, there's no alternative to building the system. So, we might as well start learning how to build successful systems, and how to make those systems work for us, folks.

So, what are the best systems out there if you decide to establish yourself as an Internet Expert, for example?

Is there a secret to an online success and how to tell what systems would help you become more successful—and which of them would only be a distraction, a waste of your time?

The secret here, folks, is to focus on the best, and ignore the rest. Just like in betting on horses. The public usually places wagers on all kinds of horses in the race, at random. But if you decide to educate yourself on the subject a little bit, if you start analyzing the trends, you will notice that only a handful of horses consistently win, over and over again.

The reason those horses win all the time is the fact that they are simply the strongest and best trained. In horse racing they are called 'favorites' because they have the best chances of winning and the public "favors" them the most because of that fact. In his Report "The New Rules of Money" Robert Kiyosaki says, *"The only way you win by diversifying at the racetrack is if the dark horse wins. I would prefer to focus and pick winners."* (Kiyosaki R., 2008)

It means that if you start betting only on favorites, i.e. on those horses whose odds of winning are consistently higher than the rest—you, in turn, will start winning more often as well!

So, the same rules apply in business, too. If you choose only a handful of winning strategies, focus on them one at a time, and master them to the point of becoming great at them—you will become very, very successful.

This is an example of 6 Most Successful and innovative systems in Internet Marketing niche that I discovered while doing a research for this book. What I want to underline here is this:

These are really the most superior, the most proven and the most successful strategic and tactical systems that can help you establish yourself as an Online Expert, establish yourself as an expert in your internet marketing niche and establish yourself as an expert in your field Globally . . . isn't THAT what we all REALLY WANT?

These systems will give you an absolute best, MAXIMUM AMOUNT OF EXPOSURE—but only if you learn them, master them and apply them correctly. Here we go:

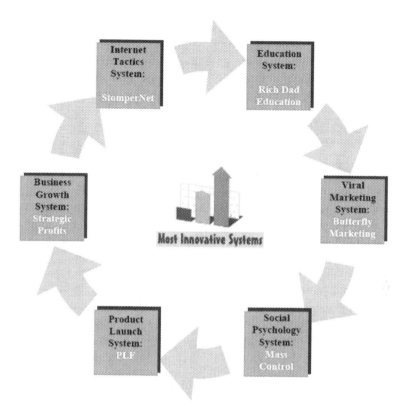

Most Innovative Systems

System # 1. **Rich Dad Education** founded by Robert Kiyosaki, an author of best-selling novel "Rich Dad, Poor Dad" that was translated in 47 different languages and sold over 26 million copies worldwide. In 1997 Robert and his wife Kim established Cashflow Technologies, in order to market their own books, games and other media. Rich Dad Education helps ordinary people, like you and I, become financially independent through the use of various tactics, such as investing in stocks and real estate, owning your own businesses, and, most importantly, by becoming "financially intelligent."

Web: www.richdadeducation.com

System # 2. **Butterfly Marketing** by Mike Filsaime. Yaro Starak said about this amazing program on his blog: " . . . *Essentially to* "butterfly market" is all about viral marketing. Viral marketing is when the marketplace itself—as in your customers and the general public—promote your product for you. It spreads "virally" without you having to proactively sell or promote beyond the initial system you set up. If you have success with viral marketing you don't need to spend money on advertising or ongoing promotion—it's set and forget." (Starak, Butterfly Marketing Manuscript Review, 2006). That's how powerful this system is, guys!

Web: www.butterflymarketing.com

System # 3. **Mass Control** by Frank Kern. Frank Kern is the mastermind behind some of the biggest launches in Internet History, for those of you who have not heard of Frank Kern, this Social Psychology Marketing system brought in over $23 Million Dollars in 24 hours, and a whopping 958,000 per hour on some of his campaigns. In a nutshell, "*Mass Control* is a way of selling without the selling part" (Tremayne, 2010), it's more about being a friend recommending a product/service to another friend without being the pushy sales person . . . on the contrary, with *Mass Control* people are literally lining up to pay you . . . FOREVER. That's why anyone will be able to use *Mass Control* because it teaches you how you can be yourself but also market very effectively at the same time . . .

Web: www.masscontrolsite.com

System # 4. **Product Launch Formula** by Jeff Walker. This is what Ray Johnson Group says about this System: "If you are serious about making money online, I mean real money online to the point where you replace your current job with online marketing, then somewhere down the line you are going to launch a product. If you want to launch your product with the maximum sales, if you want to play in the big leagues, then there is only one method that you must use, Jeff Walker's Product Launch Formula . . . a system that literally has customers so hyped and ready to buy that when you finally open the doors you get a flood of sales right off the bat. Jeff

Walker's Product Launch Formula shows you how to launch with that flood of customers." (Johnson, 2007)

Web: www.productlaunchformula.com

System # 5. **StomperNet** by Brad Fallon and Andy Jenkins. In my humble opinion, Yaro Starak was able to capture the essence of StomperNet better than anyone else when he said, *"StomperNet is the ultimate search engine optimization and website conversion course . . . Brad Fallon and Andy Jenkins are the only guys I know who specialize in SEO *and* conversion strategies and are putting together a comprehensive course on the subject. There just isn't any other course out there that teaches this stuff to the advanced level that these guys cover."* (Starak, Your Last Chance To Get Into StomperNet Is Today, 2006) No wonder their members are willing to pay $800 a month—just to stay in the program and continue learning the winning SEO and traffic conversion strategies!

Web: www.stompernet.com

System # 6. **Business Growth System** by Rich Schefren and his company, Strategic Profits (now in Strategic Alliance with StomperNet). "The Business Growth System is designed mainly for those people who want to learn how to build a sustainable business in a niche ideally suited to their strengths." (Simister, 2008).

Web: www.strategicprofits.com/coaching

Chapter 7. The First Recap

So, let's review what we've learned so far . . .

You've told me that:

No. 1.: You know that you want to achieve success.
No. 2.: You understand the concept of Values.
No. 3.: You have an Attitude of Gratitude, that is you know what you've got, you are grateful for what you've got, but you also realize that you are lacking something that lies between where you stand right now and where you are willing to be.
No. 4.: You understand that, in order to be successful, you have to have a system.

Right?

You've also asked me a question:

What are my options?

And I said to you that before we get into options discussion, you have to realize that, in order to evaluate and analyze options, you have to understand what a System is and why it is so important . . . And now, since we've gone through a concept of a System, it will be easier for us to get into options analysis—now that you are better prepared for that (I hope!)

OK, OK, I hear ya. Here's what I suggest you could do if you already know what goals you are trying to achieve, based on your own values.

Chapter 8. Success Options Chart

Here's something for you to evaluate:

Where do you stand right now?

Where do you want to be, based on your values and your goals? What is it that you are lacking, in order to achieve Success? What direction to take, in order to arrive to your destination faster? In other words, what are your Options?

Here's what I call "Success Options Chart." It is a roadmap for you, to help you see where you stand and what your Success Options are:

Here are your Success options: Study, Work, Start a Business or Retire . . . Most likely, you already belong to one or two of the categories of people that I will describe further, or you used to belong to at least one of those categories in the past.

Your Success Options

If you are a **Student** right now, you can continue to study. What you can study is Success of others, then you can try to do what they are doing and some day you may become successful, too.

If you are a **Worker**, you have to understand why you are working and how you can ultimately become more successful by working smarter—not harder.

If you are a **Business Owner** already, you have to re-evaluate why you decided to own your own business in the first place, and how you are progressing towards success.

And if you have already **Retired**, maybe reading this book will not make that much of a difference to you, as you have probably already achieved success and retired as a result of having achieved that success, right? Even still, you may just like that feeling of accomplishment, and you would love to achieve success all over again.

So, regardless of where you stand right now—keep reading!

I will tell you what my Success Option was when I was getting started.

I wanted to improve my skills and help businesses improve their Business Models.

Why? Because I wanted to gain more money, more time, more resources . . . And ultimately more freedom for myself, in order to realize my dreams.

Chapter 9. Why Complaints are Important

Now, in order to create Success in Life you have to learn how to solve problems. And, in order to solve problems, you have to listen to what people complain about.

Remember—Complaints are very important!

Why?

Because Rich Schefren taught me in one of his Profits Vault videos that *"If people complain—there is a problem. If there's a problem—there's a solution. And—if you can solve problems—you can build a business around it!"* (Schefren, Strategic Profits Vault)

So, what do you hear people complaining about the most?

This is what **Students** usually complain about:

I am getting my education, but no one would tell me how I am supposed to succeed in life AFTER I finish my education. Instead, I am left scratching my head about what to do next and how to repay the huge amount of debt they call a 'Student Loan' . . .

This is what **Workers** complain about:

After years of struggle, I finally got my job. However, no one would tell me how I am supposed to juggle my job and my personal life. Plus, as no jobs are secure these days, I constantly have to improve my skills and look for another job all the time. When I work, I have money, but I don't have time. When I am looking for work, I have enough time, but no money.

This is what **Business people** complain about:

I managed to scrape up some money and start my own business. At least, I don't have to report to anyone except my wife/husband/ business partner or government. However, I work harder than before,

I work longer hours, I am responsible for everything—from start to finish. And the profits are nowhere near to what I expected! This is not how I imagined a life of a Business owner!

Now, when it comes to **Retired people**, they seem to complain the most, and about a lot of things. But the most common thread is this one:

After years and years of hard work I finally managed to retire and decided to devote all my time to my family, my kids and my grandchildren. I started to travel and spend more time with my friends, who are also retired, for the most part. But I got bored very fast—and found out that I want to get back to work, or do some other activities! What a disappointment! I thought that retirement would bring me joy and happiness, but it only brought me a feeling of loneliness and boredom . . . I don't like it at all and I want to be active again!

So, it seems like none of these categories of people are happy to be where they are, and no one is being successful here. . . so what's the way out of this riddle?

IS SUCCESS MORE OF AN EXCEPTION THAN THE RULE?

Chapter 10. Rich Dad's Advice, 3
Questions and Business Quiz

Robert T. Kiyosaki, a renowned author and business strategist, wrote a series of books called "Rich Dad, Poor Dad". In one of them called 'Before You Quit Your Job: Ten Real-Life Lessons Every Entrepreneur Should Know About Building a Multimillion-Dollar Business' he wrote, *"The real secret to making money and reaching financial independence is not staying an employee, but starting a company and quickly developing it."* (Kiyosaki R. T., Chapter 1: What Is the Difference Between an Employee and an Entrepreneur?, 2005) Sounds pretty simple, doesn't it?

But here's the kicker. Before you decide to quit your job and start a company—would it make sense for you to look at yourself in the mirror first and answer these 3 questions:

Do you want to start a Business?
Do you have what it takes to start a Business?
Do you know what kind of business will work for you?

Take a Quiz

1) **How Much is 1 + 1?**
a) 2
b) 3
c) 10
d) 100
e) Many, if you use Power of Leverage

2) **What do you need to start a successful business?**
a) Experience
b) Desire to Succeed
c) Vision
d) Business Plan
e) All of the above

3) What is more important?
a) Knowing your Market
b) Having a Business Plan
c) Having a great Offer
d) Having great Marketing Tools
e) All of the above

4) What Business Model is the most successful?
a) Self-employed
b) Affiliate
c) Franchisee
d) Employee
e) Business Owner or Investor

5) What is the best business strategy?
a) Get a Business Loan
b) Do it yourself
c) Hire someone to do it
d) Ask an Expert to tell you how to do it
e) Create a Joint Venture with an Expert

If you've chosen "e)" as the best answer to each of the 5 questions—congratulations! If you've got at least one of them wrong—you have to agree that you are not ready yet to be an Entrepreneur and probably should consider doing something else and get prepared first, or maybe admit that being an entrepreneur is not for you . . .

OK, suppose that the test results came out in your favor, i.e. the quiz shows that you both know and have what it takes to become a successful entrepreneur and you are convinced that starting a company is the best way to go for you . . .

What kind of company, though?

How can you start a business and know that the **business model** you choose will work for you, that it will give you the financial independence, that it will help you become successful in life?

And what is a business model anyway? Huh?

Chapter 11. Business Model - Definition, Components and Types

The term *business model* describes a broad range of informal and formal models that are used by enterprises to represent various aspects of business, including its purpose, offerings, strategies, infrastructure, organizational structures, trading practices and operational processes and policies. Although the term can be traced to the 1950s, it achieved mainstream usage only in the 1990s. Many informal definitions of the term can be found in popular business literature, such as the following:

Wikipedia, the free encyclopedia: "A **business model** is a conceptual tool that contains a big set of elements and their relationships and allows expressing the business logic of a specific firm. It is a description of the value a company offers to one or several segments of customers and of the architecture of the firm and its network of partners for creating, marketing, and delivering this value and relationship capital, to generate profitable and sustainable revenue streams." (Wikipedia, Business model)

Business Model Components

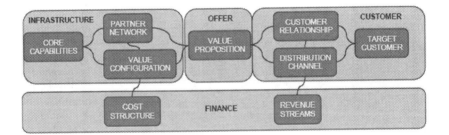

Business Model Design Template
By Dr. Alexander Osterwalder

Infrastructure

- CORE CAPABILITIES: The capabilities and competencies necessary to execute a company's business model.
- PATNER NETWORK: The business alliances which complement other aspects of the business model.
- VALUE CONFIGURATION: The rationale which makes a business mutually beneficial for a business and its customers.

Offer

- VALUE PROPOSITION: The products and services a business offers.

Customers

- TARGET CUSTOMER: The target audience for a business' products and services.
- DISTRIBUTION CHANNEL: The means by which a company delivers products and services to customers. This includes the company's marketing and distribution strategy.
- CUSTOMER RELATIONSHIP: The links a company establishes between itself and its different customer segments. The process of managing customer relationships is referred to as customer relationship management.

Finances

- COST STRUCTURE: The monetary consequences of the means employed in the business model. A company's DOC.
- REVENUE: The way a company makes money through a variety of revenue flows. A company's income.

"These 9 business model building blocks constitute a business model design template which allows companies to describe their business model." (Osterwalder, 2006)

Types of Business Models

As you can see from the Chart above, Businesses are not created equal. As a result, right off the bat—by default—the level of Success of Business owners in all these businesses is not equal either.

Let's look at each and every circle in this Chart and analyze what the Pros and Cons are when it comes to Success rate of Business owners in various types of businesses.

But first, in order to do that effectively, we need to define things that are important for your business, like Startup and Carrying costs, Control Factor, Leverage, Customer base, Growth Potential, Profitability, Replicability and Multiple Income Streams.

Let's start with definitions, so that you could understand why these things are important for your business and your own success in your business.

1. Startup Costs - expenses incurred in relation to the creation and the development of a business model.

2. Carrying Costs - expenses of living in and maintaining the business model. This includes mortgage payments, property taxes, heating, repairs, maintenance fees, etc.

3. Control - a process implemented in a business model to help in achieving specific goals.

4. Leverage - your ability of having a superior or more favorable position in a business model.

5. Customer Base - total list of customers available to a business model, as well as the total number of potential customers with specific classification or buying characteristics.

6. Growth Potential - generally, an estimation of the amount of growth yet to occur.

7. Replicability - capability of a business model to replicate itself.

8. Scalability - capability of the underlying business model to offer the potential for growth within the company.

9. Multiple Income Streams - availability of multiple ways to create income in a business model for higher profits.

10. Profitability - efficiency of a business model at generating earnings.

So, just to make it perfectly clear for you—by selecting the same parameters, we are comparing apples to apples and oranges to oranges in each and every business model that we analyze.

However, as you will also see further in this book, each particular business model has its own peculiarities, i.e. advantages, problems or constraints that either make that model more attractive, or less attractive for a business owner.

At first, let me explain to you why I needed to research and analyze Business Models—and what I found out in my case study.

Chapter 12. Business Success Blueprint

Because I did not understand the difference between various Business Models in the past, I kept making wrong decisions when selecting this or that Business Model. The fact that I am gullible by nature did not help things either. Like most people, I would easily get excited about some new business idea or opportunity and I tend to forget to ask all important questions about my success potential with that opportunity.

I tried several home businesses, a number of multi-level marketing opportunities, I have been a self-employed consultant and an investor. Regardless of the model I chose, I invariably kept failing in the end, and I could not understand why.

Finally, I decided to analyze my situation and create a **Blueprint** that would help me research, analyze and determine the effectiveness level of any business model BEFORE actually starting that business or getting involved in it.

Every time I failed at an opportunity, I was getting better at researching and analyzing it. I studied risk management and business modeling from the best experts in these fields, and I have done a lot of research on the subject of Business Models.

So by now, at this point of time, I can say that I developed a high level of expertise in this area, to the point that I can calculate the level of success of ANY business model, with an accuracy of plus/minus 10%.

That's why I called this tool "**Business Success Blueprint**".

Moreover, I am about to share this Blueprint with the rest of the world, so that anyone could measure the level of certainty of his or her success in any Business, before you even start it or get involved in it. Or, to those who are already involved in a certain business, it will help them see very clearly how effective their current business model is and how profitable it would be for them in the future if they haven't started turning the profits yet.

Most business experts agree on a theory of "thirds": Of all the new business start-ups:

1) one third eventually turns a profit,
2) one third breaks even . . . and
3) one third will never make any profit and eventually has to close down.

According to a study by the U.S. Small Business Administration, only two thirds of all small business start-ups survive during the first 2 years in operation and less than 50% make it to 5 years. Using Dunn & Bradstreet data, they found that only *"76 percent of new firms were open after two years, 47 percent after four years and 38 percent after six years."* (Headd, 2002)

Why is that? According to Rich Schefren, *"Lack of fundamental business building knowledge is really the primary cause for so much struggling and time wasting."* (Schefren, Internet Business Manifesto, 2006)

If we go even deeper and start drilling down to the very root of the problem, we will find that the business owners (and business group owners in organizations) do not understand their company's Business Models per se, and this is the **underlying reason** of why their businesses continue to fail.

To be more accurate, when we talk about Business Models and the society at large, we find 4 distinct categories of people:

Group 1
"Homo Ignoramus"

Group 1 is the **Majority of the population** that does not understand the concept of Business Models. I called this group "Homo Ignoramus"—not because I accuse the society of being ignorant, but only because, loosely translated from Latin, it simply means "*The Person that does not know.*" It's not their fault that they do not know, but there are reasons why they don't know.

So why don't they know?

Because first of all they neither own any business at all, nor they are faced with the necessity of making decisions in their business group—that's why they don't know, and they don't care.

Secondly, they have never been taught this subject at school, so how would they know any difference between let's say a "Franchise" Business Model, as opposed to an "Affiliate" Business Model? So, once they decide to get involved in this or that business, they go with their "gut feeling" and hearsay, as opposed to researching, analyzing and making decisions based on a strong knowledge of the subject. What happens as a result is that they end up choosing the wrong business, or a weak position in someone else's business, or both. They waste tons of money, time and efforts and still end up broke at the end and have to declare bankruptcy. In other words, they have to join the 50% of all businesses that fail within the first 2 to 5 years.

I also suspect that there is a third reason, (my "Conspiracy Theory", so to speak) i.e. governments and large corporations are deliberately trying to keep the knowledge about Business Models to themselves, in order to manipulate the masses and keep them in check. Maybe it was those people who invented the saying, "Ignorance is bliss"? I don't know for sure, but it's definitely something to think about . . .

I guess, there's also practical logic behind it: If everyone becomes a business owner—who is going to do all the work? Eh? ;-)

Group 2
"Busy Bodies"

As a Business Solutions Consultant in the IT Industry, I speak to a great number of business owners on a daily basis. I find that **some business owners** did study Business Models in the past, as a part of their MBA program or another post-graduate business program. However, because their study was superficial at best, they either misunderstood the concept of a Business Model, or forgot what they actually learned about the subject. So they end up the same way as the first category of people. They end up with a weak business model at best, and they keep wondering why they are working so hard, and achieving so little.

As Rich Schefren pointed out in one of his reports, **"Busy, busy, bankrupt, dead"** (Schefren, The Entrepreneurial Emergency, 2008) becomes their life formula. Instead of seeking help, they continue suffering, stuck in an endless nightmare of a vicious circle that they're in.

Group 3
"The Nutty Professors"

There are some **smart theoreticians** out there who have great understanding of the constituents and concepts of Business Models, but who get totally confused when facing necessity to analyze the performance of an actual Business Model in an organization, especially when it comes to its effectiveness and profitability. In most cases, these theoreticians are not business owners themselves, so their theoretical knowledge is useless for the actual business.

So their knowledge does not really benefit the "Busy bodies", the type of business owners I've described earlier.

I called them "The Nutty Professors" because this is how they are being perceived by society. I admit that sometimes I am being perceived and even feel like one, too, being stuck in the "Twilight Zone" of my own secret thoughts, unable to practically apply my observations or to share them with the world . . . One colleague of mine even called me a "A Mad Scientist" which, I guess is just a variety of a Nutty Professor who has not achieved his mastery level yet . . . ☺

Group 4
"The Top Experts"

There is a very **small group of practitioners** (literally, a handful of them in a whole world!) that are actually great at both defining the structure and determining the flow in the delivery chains of the specific business models. These practitioners are indeed the "Top Experts" for the public, private and non profit sector. Their teachings are adopted by highest levels or governments and "Fortune 500" companies alike. These practitioners are the "elite few" that understand the Business Models of the world's largest business organizations and they continue consulting their owners on how to make their business models more effective, productive and profitable.

However, even if business owners allow the best consultants come in and conduct the most thorough analysis within their business or business group, because of the abstract nature of a Business Model, the decision makers are still not receiving full value of that analysis. They are still not receiving the actual **measurable and specific results** of their Business Model analysis, due to lack of _measurement tools_ and _effectiveness indicators_ that eventually determine success or failure of a given Business Model. The complexity and multiplicity of modern-day delivery chains in government and large corporations does not make things easier for the analysts either. And their conclusions leave business owners and business group owners even more confused and unhappy after the analysis is completed.

So I had to develop my own measurement tools and effectiveness indicators, in order to see my own success rate in any given Business Model.

What am I talking about?

Well, let's analyze and compare various types of Business Models, as well as their Pros, Cons and Effectiveness of each model—and you will see for yourself.

Chapter 13. The Pros and Cons of "Self-employment" Business Model

Pros: 5

Cons: 5

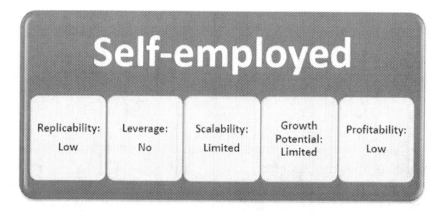

What is Self-Employment?

Self-employed is a person who works for himself/herself instead of being an employee of another person or organization, drawing income from a trade or business. (Wikipedia, Self-employment, 2010)

Who belongs to this category?
Consultants, Doctors, Lawyers, Accountants, etc.

Analysis "As you join [the ranks of self-employed - VS], dreaming of setting your own schedule and choosing your own projects, remember that the pros and cons of self-employment are often two sides of the same coin. Independent people, like you, often relish the idea of owning a business and not having a boss.

However, every client will become your boss—as will the banks and other people who provide you with funding or credit to get your business going. Another commonly cited plus to running a business is the freedom of flexible hours. In reality, you will be putting in more than full-time hours for at least the first year, as you get your business off the ground.

It is also important to remember it takes more than enthusiasm and a business concept to become sustainably self-employed." (Kristolaitis, 2006)

The biggest confusion and misconception about this business model is that most people do not understand the difference between business ownership and being self-employed. The only person who managed to articulate the difference between these two very clearly was Rich Schefren. This is what one of Rich's students said about one of Rich's most famous and profound reports called "Internet Business Manifesto": "Possibly one of the most valuable lessons you'll learn from Rich is the difference between self-employment and business ownership.

With employment or self-employment you are trading your time for money, and you are doing all the work. Because you have limited time, there's only so much work you can do and a very limited amount of money you can make. You're stuck! Want to grow your income, you can't because you're too busy working in it rather than on it. This is the plight of many do-it-yourselfers, work-at-homers, and small "business" owners." - Chris Rizzo "What I've Learned From Internet Business Coach Rich Schefren."

Level of Effectiveness of "Self-Employed" Business Model

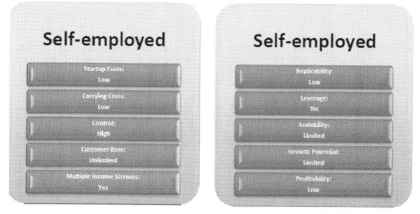

Self-employed	Self-employed
Startup Costs: Low	Replicability: Low
Carrying Costs: Low	Leverage: No
Control: High	Scalability: Limited
Customer Base: Unlimited	Growth Potential: Limited
Multiple Income Streams: Yes	Profitability: Low

Pros: 5	Cons: 5

Level of Effectiveness = 50%

Book One "Success - An Art or a Science?"

Chapter 14. The Pros and Cons of "Affiliate Marketing" Business Model

Pros: 5

Cons: 5

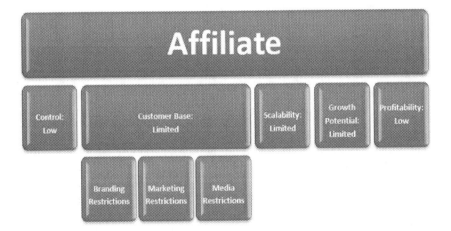

What is Affiliate Marketing?

Affiliate marketing is a web-based marketing practice in which a business rewards one or more affiliates for each visitor or customer brought about by the affiliate's marketing efforts. (Wikipedia, Affiliate Marketing, 2010)

Who belongs to this category?

Internet Marketers, Independent Associates, Independent Distributors, Agents, etc.

Analysis

An affiliate program is a very simple way for a merchant to outsource sales. The merchant only pays a commission when a sale is made, and the affiliate only has to promote the product without being concerned about delivery or customer support.

One of the examples of an affiliate program is Internet Marketing.

"Pros and Cons of Internet Marketing"
(An Article by nPresence Resources)

"Internet marketing is the talk of the town. Businesses, whether old or new, see the importance of internet marketing. For the past few years, internet marketing has made its mark in terms of providing successful online presence. But just like all things, internet marketing has its downsides as well. Let's take a closer look at the advantages of internet marketing. In the same manner, let us point out some of the disadvantages of internet marketing.

Advantages of Internet Marketing

Internet marketing has several known advantages. Internet marketing experts look at internet marketing as the primary solution to online presence. Here are some of the advantages of internet marketing:

- Internet marketing is a low cost promotional strategy.

  Internet marketing, unlike other business, requires no big capital. Internet marketing does not demand so much investment. It doesn't need any physical capital since internet is purely online.

- Internet marketing is the easiest way to reach a global market.

  Internet marketing does not limit your business to a particular location. Since internet reaches all parts of the world, internet marketers can also reach a worldwide target market. Therefore, internet marketing gives online business a higher chance of success.

- Internet marketing reaches target market easily.

  Internet marketing can reach a target market in an instant. In the same manner, potential customers can reach your online business as quickly as one click. Therefore, internet marketing makes online business move fast.

Disadvantages of Internet Marketing

Internet marketing has its downside as well. Although it is true that there are more advantages in internet marketing rather than its disadvantages, it is always worth a time to go over some of the disadvantages of internet marketing.

- Internet Marketing does not build trust instantly.

Internet marketing is something that exists on the web. It is difficult to tell whether something is good or not because there are no physical evidences. It takes time for an internet marketer to gain the trust of online users.

- *Internet marketing is a tough competition.*

  Because of the many benefits of internet marketing, there are so many business oriented people who became interested. As a result, there is an overload of information presented on the internet. To make your own information stand out, you need to keep up with the tough competition.

Now that you know the advantages and disadvantages of internet marketing, think twice before you jump off being an internet marketer yourself. It pays to think about it first so you'll save the possible waste of time and effort. Overall, internet marketing is good as long as you know how to do it right." (Resources, 2007)

*   *   *

"If you've been looking for online opportunities, then you already know that you can spend $1,000, $3,000 or even $5,000 to learn how to make money using sites like Google, eBay, or through affiliate marketing.

The problem with using them is that you always have to stay one-step ahead of the changes, one-step ahead of the competition, and try to guess the whims of greedy corporate executives.

Just like I lost my cash flow overnight, you could too. So, why invest your time and your hard-earned money in something that could be useless tomorrow?" (Dr. Bradley Semp, Creator of Cashmaps)

Level of Effectiveness of "Affiliate" Business Model

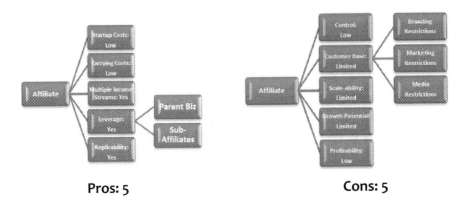

Pros: 5   Cons: 5

Level of Effectiveness = 50%

Chapter 15. The Pros and Cons of a Franchise Ownership

Pros: 1

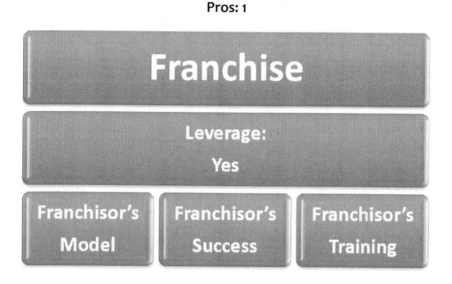

Franchise

Leverage: Yes

| Franchisor's Model | Franchisor's Success | Franchisor's Training |

Cons: 9

Franchise

| Control: No | Customer Base: Limited | Startup Costs: High | Carrying Costs: High | Scalability: No | Growth Potential: Limited | Replic- ability: No | Multiple Income Streams: No | Profit- ability: Limited |

What is Franchising?

Franchising (from the French *franc* for honesty or freedom)
is a method of doing business wherein a "franchisor"
authorizes proven methods of doing business to a
"franchisee" for a fee and a percentage of sales or profits.

Who belongs to this category?

*Any type of a Franchise Owner ("franchisee")
if you are not a Franchisor*

Analysis

What is a franchise? It's a legal and commercial relationship between the owner of a trademark, service mark, brand name, or advertising symbol (the franchisor) and an individual or organization (the franchisee) wishing to use that identification in a business. The franchise governs the method of conducting business between the two parties. Generally, a franchisee sells goods or services supplied by the franchisor or that meet the franchisor's quality standards.

Think of franchising—or at least the costs of it—as paying for the work someone else has already done in developing a successful business model, marketing strategy, and superior operations efficiencies.

The popularity of the franchise business model has to do with its proven track record of success and ease in becoming a business owner; however, while the success rate for franchise-owned businesses is significantly higher than for independent businesses, no individual franchise is guaranteed to succeed.

"Of all the "systems" out there, the franchises were "supposed" to be the most profitable. They normally cost $200,000 to start (on the

low-end) and only promise to make $50,000 per year. So, it would take 4 years just to pay back the initial investment.

In other words, I'd have to work 4 years for FREE. Isn't that crazy? Plus, I don't know many people who have an extra $200k under their sofa cushions to follow those systems. I just couldn't see why someone would want to buy themselves a JOB and deal with the headache that comes with it." (Ty Coughlin, Hawaii)

* * *

Experts state that 40 cents of every retail or service dollar spent by consumers is spent in a franchised business. In 2000, most analysts estimated that franchising companies and their franchisees accounted for $1 trillion in annual U.S. retail sales, with approximately one out of every 12 U.S. retail business establishments is a franchised business. A new franchise business opens every 8 minutes of every business day.

"In a recent national survey of one thousand franchisees from forty-eight separate franchise companies, 44 percent would not have purchased their franchise if they had known then what they know now.

Forty-six percent would not recommend their franchise to a close friend or family member, and 53 percent do not consider their franchise business to be a financial success! The research results clearly show that our industry has some work to do in the area of franchise relations." (Jeff Johnson of Johnson Franchise Consulting Inc.)

* * *

"Why would anybody go out and spend $50,000 on a franchise to make whatever when you can just start a business with no capital out of pocket and way more scalable?" (Brad Fallon, a Co-founder of StomperNet)

"Do Entrepreneurs own Franchises?

Most of the popular franchises purposefully screen out entrepreneurs. They don't want entrepreneurs because past experience shows that entrepreneurs are less likely to follow the system. Entrepreneurs will always like to tweak and improve the system." (Rich Schefren of Strategic Profits)

Level of Effectiveness of "Franchise" Business Model

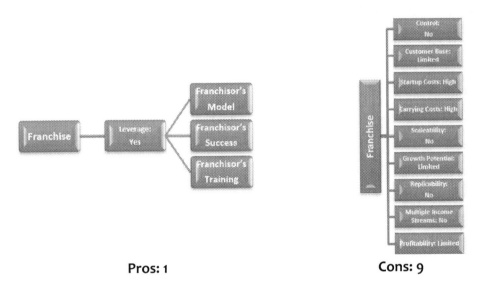

Pros: 1   Cons: 9

Level of Effectiveness = 10%

You're probably thinking: "It can't be right. If Franchising model is only 10% effective—how come it still works? What about McDonald's, Starbucks, and other franchises that are successful, thriving and "proven"?"

My answer to this is threefold:

1) It is not the Model itself that is 10% effective. It is YOUR level of success in that model that is only 10% effective;

2) Because you don't own the Franchise—Franchisor does, your level of success simply can't be same as the Franchisor's;

3) As it is stated in Nazeer Daud's article "Six Reasons Why Business Franchising Works":

" . . . As you [The Franchisor, that is—VS] take on more franchisees, you make more money from licensing, and although franchisees may damage a franchisee's profitability, it will not damage total revenue, and therefore you will continue to prosper even if your franchisees struggle." (Daud, 2008)

You can see from the above quote that, by design itself, **the Franchisor** is the one whose revenue is protected in this model, and the risk is assumed by the franchisees.

So, what is the Effectiveness level of a Franchisor who turns out to be the real "Business Owner" in this model?

Read the next Chapter, my friends—and you will see.

Chapter 16. The Pros and Cons of Business Ownership

Pros: 8

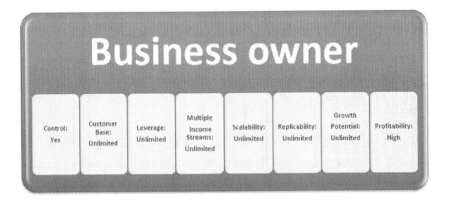

Cons:2

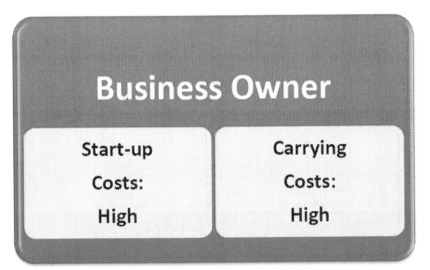

What is Business Ownership?

Business ownership is any type of Business that you own, but not manage yourself.

Who belongs to this category?

Any type of a Business Owner that is not directly involved in managing his/her business.

Analysis

Advantages of Business Ownership

The highest leverage is achieved by multiplying multiple efforts of multiple resources—people, time and money—to maximize business objectives and create more value. Business Ownership provides the ultimate freedom for the owner.

Disadvantages of Business Ownership

Start-up and operating costs are very high.

Business Ownership requires outstanding vision and 'uncommon sense', in order to gain and sustain consistent growth and maintain competitive advantage.

Level of Effectiveness of "Business Ownership" Model

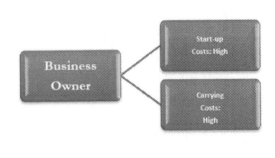

Pros:8   Cons:2

Level of Effectiveness = 80%

Chapter 17. The Pros and Cons of Being An Investor

Pros: 8

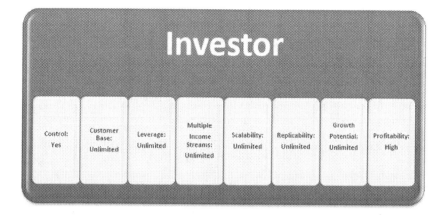

Cons: 2

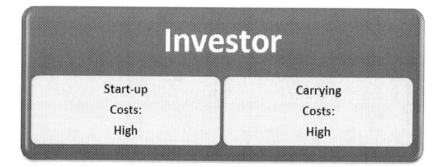

What is Investing?

Investing is any type of Investment Business where you do not own the assets you invest in.

Who belongs to this category?

Stock Traders, Forex Traders, Real Estate Investors, etc.

Analysis

Advantages of Investing

According to Merrill Lynch and Cap Gemini World Wealth Report, *"The world's population of high net worth individuals (HNWIs) [in simple terms—**number of rich people**—VS] grew 17.1% to 10.0 million in 2009. HNWI financial wealth increased 18.9% from 2008 levels to $39 trillion. After losing 24.0% in 2008, Ultra-HNWIs saw wealth rebound 21.5% in 2009.*

With financial markets still in flux, some of these [rich people] indicated they are approaching their passion investments as "investor-collectors", seeking out those items that are perceived to have tangible long-term value." (Gemini, 2010)

What kind of items, you wonder?

Well, according to Noland Carter, chief investment officer at boutique wealth manager at Heartwood Wealth, a UK-based Financial Advisory firm *"At a time of financial insecurity, there is a natural desire to own physical assets. The pleasure gained from owning a well-made vintage car or a painstakingly constructed painting is a bonus. The stress of participating in financial markets has caused some to look elsewhere for returns in the widest sense, including enjoyment."*

"Sales of vintage cars, old jewels, derelict warships and 17th-century broadswords have broken records this year—suggesting nostalgia among the wealthy is growing.

North America remains the single largest home to HNWIs representing at 31% of the global HNWI population or 3.1 million. Asia-Pacific's HNWI population reached 3 million in 2009, matching that of Europe for the first time. Asia-Pacific wealth rose 30.9% to $9.7 trillion, surpassing the $9.5 trillion in wealth held by Europe's HNWIs." (Gemini, 2010)

Disadvantages of Investing

In his famous book "The Cashflow Quadrant" Robert T. Kiyosaki wrote,

"Being an investor may seem to be a lucrative business, but there is always a danger of making a mistake while calculating your ROI (Return On Investment). Microsoft and other companies even had to come up with special software tools that help investors calculate their ROI and alert them in case the market crashes or takes a sudden nose-dive." (Kiyosaki R. T., Cashflow Quadrant: Rich Dad's Guide to Financial Freedom, 2000)

But even with all the help, tools and information available out there, the chances of succeeding in Investment Business are not that high, mostly due to the fact that there's too much hype and proliferation of numerous myths and downright lies that surround this business. Donald Trump wrote in his New York Times Bestseller "*Think Like a Billionaire*":

"Real estate can afford great opportunities through mortgaging, leverage, and possibly even absentee management, but don't bet on it. Like anything else, it requires caution, devotion, hard work, and some luck . . . Care and study are required.

Anyone who has seen those commercials on TV in the middle of the night where individuals claim to have retired to Hawaii on the basis of real estate purchased, sold or rented should realize that the people

who sell these courses make more money from selling the courses than they do from selling any real estate or mortgaging. Those infomercials never tell you about the mountain of problems that can be associated with the ownership of real estate." (Donald J. Trump, 2004)

The San Diego Union-Tribune called this book "Required reading for serious realty investors" for a reason. Having gone through all the trials and tribulations of a Real Estate mogul, Donald is trying to caution those who are just starting their career as investors in Real Estate and stress the fact that one should carry out all necessary research and study before engaging in any real estate transactions.

Level of Effectiveness of "Investing Business" Model

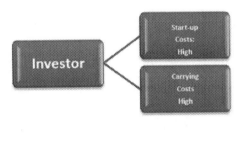

Pros: 8   Cons: 2

Level of Effectiveness = 80%

We can't change what happens to us, we can only change how we react to it. Our reaction to those events that occur in our life are directly impacted by this philosophy and this is why it is so crucial for us to never stop looking at successful models of past and present.

Chapter 18. Business Effectiveness Survey

Let's get back to "Business Success Blueprint" that I described to you in Chapter 12 of this book. If you remember, I told you that I was trying to develop a tool for myself, the one that would help me research, analyze and determine the effectiveness level of any business model EVEN BEFORE starting that business or getting involved in it.

So, in order to test the results of the Blueprint, I decided to create a "Business Effectiveness Survey" with 10 questions in it and send it out to 100 randomly chosen Franchises, MLMs, Investment firms and Home Based Businesses in North America, Europe and Australia. Here it is . . .

THE SURVEY

Question 1. Are there any Start-up Costs involved?	99% responded "Yes". Only 1 respondent said "No", but mentioned that the only way to make money in this business was through earning commissions. The owner responded: "The business is owned privately and is currently not a franchise." The Start-up costs varied between $60 and $500,000 and included Set up fees, Web site fees and minimal purchase of products. So I had to introduce "Low", "Medium" and "High" Levels of Entry, in order to make this effectiveness indicator more accurate in measuring the overall performance of the model under study.

Question 2. Are there any Ongoing Costs involved?	100% responded "Yes". But the Ongoing costs varied between $19.99 and $7,500 per month. Some respondents mentioned minimum monthly purchase of products, in order to maintain "active status" in that business. Besides, some also mentioned annual Licensing renewal fees of as high as $497. I had to apply the same "Low", "Medium" and "High" levels to this performance indicator as in Question 1.
Question 3. Will I have any Control in this business through partnership, shares or stock options?	Most respondents said "No". But one said "Yes" and mentioned that "You will be set up as a Licensee" with that particular opportunity I still had to qualify this response as a "No", as a term "Licensee" describes a person who is conducting business "on the property of another", but it does not create any control opportunity for that person to have any stake of ownership in that Company.

Question 4. Will I have any Branding, Marketing, Advertising, PR or Hiring restrictions?	This is where it actually gets interesting, and I would like to quote some of the answers here, and let you decide about the level of truthfulness of the respondents: **"Minimal restrictions."** **"Company needs to approve any materials before circulation."** **"Marketing Compliance Review."** **"You won't be restricted, but there will be usage guidelines for the branding."** **"there are few restrictions, generally very open."** Because the level of these restrictions is difficult to quantify, I had to come up with the terms "Limited" vs "Unlimited" that would automatically move this effectiveness indicator into a "Pro" or "Con" (Plus or Minus) category.

Question 5. Will I have any Customer base development restrictions?	**100% responded "No" or "Minimal restrictions".** To me, this response was not truthful enough, as I know for a fact that there is a finite number of prospects in every market. That's why I could not automatically appoint 10% to this effectiveness indicator, even if the respondent's response was negative.
Question 6. Are there any limitations to this opportunity's Growth Potential?	**100% responded "No" or "No Limit".** Again, to me, this response did not sound like a responsible answer, so I could not take it for granted. Both you and I know that there are all kinds of internal and external factors that influence growth potential of an opportunity, such as: Lack of resources, laziness and procrastination, licensing restrictions, market saturation, etc. Again, dislodging any of these factors would be irresponsible, so I could not automatically place this effectiveness indicator into a "Pro" or "Plus" category, just based on a negative answer of the respondents.

Question 7. Are there any limitations to replicating this business opportunity elsewhere?	The majority answered "No". However, one said "No" and added, **"You have the ability to hire agents and earn mlm commissions."** Another one said "Yes", and added, **"Not really sure what your intent is. Please contact us to discuss."** Only one actually understood what I was asking and said, **"Primarily open to USA, Canada, Aus, NZ, England".** The truth of the matter is, there are a number of restrictions to replicating one opportunity in different countries, for instance a Casino business would be perfectly OK in Canada or USA, but absolutely unacceptable in a Moslem country. Another conclusion drawn from the survey was that the business owners took this question too lightly or completely misunderstood what was asked.

Question 8. Are there any scalability restrictions for this opportunity?	The majority answered "No". However, one said "Yes" and added, **"Each Licensee is assigned a 100% protected territory which is expandable. Ask us for more information."**
Question 9. Is there a Multitude of ways to make money in this opportunity?	This question actually brought much more optimistic responses, such as: **"You will have access to multiple services, multiple products, and an online component."** **"Energy, Healthcare, Legal, Home Warranty, Computer tech and shopping discount."** **"We have various ways to grow your business."** **"Residential/Small Business/Employee Affinity Programs / MLM."** **"2 Tiers of commissions for Approved Business program plus commissions on new Products."** **"Can choose various 'strategies' to grow your business."** Despite such a variety of different ways to make money, I was not that impressed. To me, it only meant that the Business owners were just repeating what was promised to them by other Business owners, like them, and an opportunity to make money in different ways was clouding the real truth in these opportunities.

Question 10. Will it take long to see High Profits in this opportunity?	Drumroll, please. Here's where the real truth I mentioned earlier really came out. So, even though the majority of the respondents said, "No", some of those that said "Yes" were very revealing indeed: **"I believe you should be able to recoup your original investment within 12-24 months." (Break even)** **"It will realistically take anywhere from 2 to 4+ months before you start seeing 'high' profits." (Turn over Profits)** **"It's not an overnight get rich plan. It will take 2 to 4 years to get a high income. Is that 'long'?"** **"With current economic factors, and without knowing an individual's commitment level, we cannot project when and if high profits will be realized." (Never turn Profits at all)** Now, do you see where the theory of "thirds" really proves itself to be useful? ;-)

Chapter 19. How to Calculate Effectiveness of a Business Model

If you take all answers from the Survey—both positive and negative as 100%, here's how you calculate the model Effectiveness:

Question 1. Are there any Start-up Costs involved?

Deduct 5% for "Low" level of entry
Deduct 10% for "Medium" level of entry
Deduct 15% for "High" level of entry

Do not deduct anything if the answer was "No"

For example:

The Start-up cost is $60

Deduct 5% for "Low" level of entry

The Start-up cost is $500,000

Deduct 15% for "High" level of entry

Anything in between

Deduct 10% for "Medium" level of entry

Question 2. Are there any Ongoing Costs involved?

The same rule applies to Question 2:

From the total percentage you arrived at in Question 1, deduct 5% more if the ongoing costs are low, deduct 15% if the ongoing costs are high and deduct 10% for anything in between.

Do not deduct anything if the answer was "No"

© 2014 Val A. Slastnikov   "The Secret Power of An Expert"
Book One "Success - An Art or a Science?"

For example:

The Ongoing costs are $19.99 per month.

The ongoing costs are low. Deduct 5%.

The Ongoing costs are $7,500 per month, plus annual Licensing fees.

The ongoing costs are high. Deduct 15%.

Anything in between

Deduct 10%.

Question 3. Will I have any Control in this business through partnership, shares or stock options?

If the answer was "No", deduct 10% from what you arrived at in Question 2.

Do not deduct anything if the answer was "Yes"

Question 4. Will I have any Branding, Marketing, Advertising, PR or Hiring restrictions?

If the answer was "Yes", deduct 10% from what you arrived at in Question 3.

Do not deduct anything if the answer was "No". However, if you think that the owner was untruthful to you and there might be some sort of business restrictions after all (say, you can't advertise this opportunity on TV, or you can't approach media directly due to branding restrictions), you must still deduct 10%.

Question 5. Will I have any Customer base development restrictions?

If the answer was "Yes", deduct 10% from what you arrived at in Question 4.

Do not deduct anything if the answer was "No". However, if you think that the owner was untruthful to you and there might be some Customer base restrictions after all (say, due to territorial restrictions or licensing necessary to carry out the business), you must still deduct 10%.

Question 6. Are there any limitations to this opportunity's Growth Potential?

Same rule applies, as in Questions 4 and 5:

If the answer was "Yes", deduct 10% from what you arrived at in Question 5.

Do not deduct anything if the answer was "No". However, if you think that the owner was untruthful to you and there might be some limitations to growing your business in your area, you must still deduct 10%.

Do additional research and due diligence necessary, in order to determine if there might be some potential barriers to this opportunity growth. For instance—how many local, national and international competitors will you have?

Question 7. Are there any limitations to replicating this business opportunity elsewhere?

Same rule applies, as in Questions 4, 5 and 6:

If the answer was "Yes", deduct 10% from what you arrived at in Question 6.

Do not deduct anything if the answer was "No". However, if you think there might be some limitations to replicating this opportunity in other areas, regions or countries, you must still deduct 10%.

Again, it is your responsibility to do additional research and due diligence. Do not take any answers "at face value" because it is YOUR success that is on the line here—not the opportunity providers'

Question 8. Are there any scalability restrictions for this opportunity?

Same rule applies, as in Questions 4, 5, 6 and 7:

If the answer was "Yes", deduct 10% from what you arrived at in Question 7.

Do not deduct anything if the answer was "No". However, if you think that you may have some scalability issues down the road, you must still deduct 10%.

Question 9. Is there a Multitude of ways to make money in this opportunity?

This is a "trick question" that allows you to evaluate truthfulness of the respondents, such as:

If the answer was "No", deduct 10% from what you arrived at in Question 8.

Do not deduct anything if the answer was "Yes". However, if you think that the answers were not clear enough or not specific enough, you must still deduct 10%.

Be especially careful when the owner starts talking about various "tiers" or "levels" in the opportunity. Ask them how long will it take to get to this or that level or tier, and what level they were currently at, and how long it took them to get there.

This way you will be able to get much clearer picture for yourself.

© 2014 Val A. Slastnikov   "The Secret Power of An Expert"
Book One "Success - An Art or a Science?"

Question 10. Will it take long to see High Profits in this opportunity?

Do not take simple "No" as a valid answer to this question. Ask for clarification of what the owners consider to be "High Profits" and how soon would you be able to "break even" and start receiving profits yourself.

"2-3 days and $5000 a month" would be probably good to hear, and you don't need to deduct any points in this case.

However, "2-3 years and $50 a month" would probably mean that you should deduct 10% or more from the Sum Total and stay away from this opportunity altogether.

Takeaways

So what was the point of our exercise? What were we trying to achieve by putting together the Survey, then sending it to the business owners and then analyzing their responses?

#1. We tried to check if my Business Models Blueprint works in real life. We found out that it does.

#2. We tried to see if we could learn how to "Judge the book by its cover", i.e. if we could evaluate a Business Model without actually going into details about the business itself. We found out that we could.

#3. We tried to eliminate "Emotional Aspect" from the equation. I told you at the beginning that I was gullible. Because I was gullible, I used to get easily excited about a particular business opportunity and forgot to ask all important questions and get all important facts. We found out that it was possible to do that if we used the same Blueprint for evaluation.

#4. As an added value, we've learned that, by applying the Blueprint as a rule, we can actually read "between the lines", and interpret the responses even when the truth was omitted or concealed.

Chapter 20. The "Three Whales" of Planning

If you don't design your own life plan, chances are you'll fall into someone else's plan. And guess what they have planned for you? Not much."

- Jim Rohn (Rohn)

Rich Schefren said, *"There's opportunistic thinking and strategic thinking."* (Schefren, Internet Business Manifesto, 2006)

The best way to outline your strategy is to constantly work on your Business Plan. Yes, guys. I strongly believe that putting together a strong Business Plan and then continuously refining it is not a one time event, but a meticulous and ongoing process. It has more to do with overall planning of your whole business than anything else.

Now—what is Planning?

Planning is the start of the process by which you turn empty dreams into achievements. It helps you avoid the trap of working extremely hard but achieving little.

Planning's main goal is to help you achieve the maximum effect from a given effort.

The process helps you to:

- Take stock of your current position
- Identify precisely what is to be achieved
- Work out the process of getting there in the most effective, efficient way possible.
- Detail precisely and cost figure the who, what, when, where, why and how of achieving your target.
- Assess the impact of your plan on your organization and the people within it, and on the outside world.
- Evaluate whether the effort, costs and implications of achieving your plan are worth the achievement

- Consider the control mechanisms, whether reporting, quality or cost control, etc. that are needed to achieve your plan and keep it on course.

You may have heard of one approach to the Pareto principle: that 80% of a job is completed in 20% of the time. Another application in a non-planning environment is that 80% of the effort tends to achieve 20% of the results. By thinking and planning we can reverse this to 20% of the effort achieving 80% of the results. We may even decide that it is more efficient not to attempt the remaining work at all!

What is Strategic Planning?

According to Wikipedia, "**Strategic planning** *is a process of defining strategy, or direction, and making decisions on allocating resources to pursue this strategy, including the capital and people.*" (Wikipedia, Strategic Planning, 2010)

To paraphrase this, before you start doing a "Step by step" planning of your business, you have to think on a larger scale first.

You see, "Strategic planning" and "Business planning" is not the same thing, and unfortunately most of the people do not know the difference between the two. Strategy is an overall direction of where you are planning to take your life and business in the long run, and it goes way beyond just your business plan. It involves a lot of soul-searching and seeking out the ultimate goal, the 3 Big Whales of planning, which are:

- The BIG WHAT
- The BIG WHY and
- The BIG HOW

In other words you have to think on a BIG LEVEL when you are crafting your ultimate goals, and you have to be able to answer the BIG QUESTIONS first, way before you start writing your Business Plan.

Just like a builder first lays the foundation for the house, you must also start with the foundation.

So let me break it down for you in 3 very easy steps.

In previous chapters we've talked about Success options and how selecting this or that model for your business may seriously affect your level of success in your life and business.

So please be careful and think long and hard about your success options and the model that you choose.

But, once you decide on these two, you have to be careful once again. Because the next step deals with the design and with building the foundation for your future.

Again, I suggest you try to understand the BIG WHAT first. In other words—what is it that you are ultimately trying to achieve?

THE BIG WHAT

Believe it or not, but I spoke to many people in my consulting career, and you'll be surprised how many people do not have any idea of what they are ultimately trying to achieve in their lives, whether it comes to their relationships with others, or when it comes to their professional careers, their business development or their final destination, such as retirement planning.

What we are talking about here is a Social disease called "Lack of Vision." And I'm not talking here about lack of our ability to see things clearly. I'm talking about lack of our ability to clearly see the ultimate goal.

As per Wikipedia, *"Vision defines an intended or desired future state"* of things. Wikipedia says that, *"in order to know where we're going we need to know exactly where we stand, then determine where we want to go and how to get there"*. (Wikipedia, Strategic Planning, 2010)

No, I'm not blaming people for showing symptoms of this disease in everything they do, as "Vision development" is not one of the subjects that they teach us at school—even though I think they should!

Why is it so difficult for us to develop the Vision? Well, because it has something to do with our future. And we all know that deep down inside we are all afraid of looking into our future, we all live in denial, just "hoping" that tomorrow will be better than today, but doing very little in terms of trying to change our future.

Well, as one of my former superiors used to say, "*Hope is not a strategy!*"

And when it comes to planning, most people only distinguish between Strategy and Tactics. But the underlying problem lies way deeper than that.

So . . . how do we develop our Vision?

You know what? I will probably surprise you if I say that defining your Vision is easier than you think.

THE BIG WHY

First off, we've already established that, in order to know where we're going we need to know exactly where we stand, then determine where we want to go and how to get there.

In other words, in order to determine the BIG WHAT, we need to ask the BIG WHY question.

In other words, we have to come up with the Mission statement.

Wikipedia says that "**Mission** . . . *defines the fundamental purpose of an organization or an enterprise, basically describing why it exists.*" (Wikipedia, Strategic Planning, 2010)

Do we know why we exist? I bet you that no one really knows why, otherwise we would not have so many various philosophies, religions and science theories all trying to speculate on this particular question.

What is the Mission Statement? It is basically a short written statement of the purpose of your business. In other words, your company's Mission Statement IS the BIG WHY.

THE BIG HOW

In one of Rich Schefren's most famous videos called "The Internet Business Process" Rich was talking about the role of the CEO in a business. He said that you, as a CEO of your business should be focused on THE WHAT. And let your employees bother about the BIG HOW.

According to Donald Trump, leadership is all about CONTROL AND POWER. The way I understand it is that you, as an expert, should focus on the overall guidance, i.e. only monitor and control the activities in your business and let other experts you've partnered with do the execution part.

'Paralysis by Planning'

Sometimes the planning process can be used as a method of procrastination—people may fall into the trap of prolonging the planning process to avoid having to take the first step or risk in the execution of the plan. Remember that planning is an investment—you should not invest more than you have to!

Jeff Walker, a famous author of The Product Launch Formula, said once that he never uses the term "Resolution" (as in 'New Year's Resolution', of course). He thinks that "99.9% of the "resolutions" that are made at New Years are forgotten by the middle of January." Or, like Derek Gehl, the CEO of "Internet Marketing Center" used to say, "It goes in one year—and into another!" What he is talking about, and what all strategic thinking business leaders are suggesting is this:

"Getting a vision for the life you want, and then designing a plan to achieve that life."

Chapter 21. The Experts Market

I already said at the beginning of this book that I have a tremendous empathy for Experts, my target market and that I was personally involved with Experts helping them promote themselves to prospective clients for more than 10 years now.

Within the course of those years I've been able to do a lot of soul-searching and gradually developed a great degree of awareness of what my strengths and what my weaknesses are. As my biggest strengths are research and analysis, I have been researching and analyzing Experts for the last 10 years.

I also have a background in linguistics, which is a science that studies languages. That's why I always enjoyed analyzing where the meanings of various words came from. For instance, I found out that, according to the dictionary, *"An Expert is a person with a high degree of skill in or knowledge of a certain subject."* (Farlex, 2010)

The word "Expert" derives from Latin 'Expertus' and means "to try, test, experience or prove."

What I found out from my experience as a Recruiter in Information Technology was that the majority of experts were working too hard, but achieving too little. Instead of trying to focus on their core competence and then start positioning themselves in their target markets, most experts work with one client at a time, and then spend a lot of time and energy on trying to find the next project.

So back in 2007 I created my first Free Report "How To Hire An IT Expert", hoping to change my client's perception about experts.

Later, working as an IT Business Solutions Consultant, I came to another stunning realization. I found out that my clients, from the smallest "Mom and Pop" shops to top Fortune 500s also did things totally wrong when it comes to understanding the buyer psychology.

Until this day most of them are still using very old, outdated Sales and Marketing methods that no longer work in the new Millennium.

So in the Summer of 2008 I created my second Free Report called "Buying Model 3G", aiming to change the client's perception about modern-day buyers.

Also, through my many years of research I found out that there is a huge Market of Experts out there and now I believe that I can help that Market in more ways than one.

IS THERE REALLY A GLOBAL MARKET FOR EXPERTS OUT THERE AND HOW BIG IS THAT MARKET?

I looked at Expert Statistics for the first time in June of 2008 and found out that Google search pulled 329 Million websites that contained the word 'expert' in them. I also searched books for and about experts on Amazon.com and it showed 402,512 results!

I did another search in February 2009. At that time Amazon.com showed 479,776 results, which proved to me that we are dealing with the fast- growing, dynamic market.

As of June 2008, there were 197,000 videos with the word "Expert" on YouTube. As of February 2009, the number of videos has increased to 305,000. That's 108,000 more in only 7 months!

I did another search in November 2010. This time the YouTube search returned Millions of results! I said to myself, "*Wow, I am definitely onto something else here!*"

Here's the table I put together from my "YouTube research" project. It shows how many experts I was able to find in each category:

- Movie Experts (60,700)
- Gaming Experts (22,100)
- Music Experts (7,710)

- Business Experts (4,050)
- Health Experts (2,890)
- Car Experts (2,560)
- Book Experts (2,550)
- Marketing Experts (2,100)
- Internet Experts (2,020)
- Fitness Experts (1,930)
- Trading Experts (1,720)
- Animal Experts (1,680)
- Sales Experts (1,670)
- Family Experts (1,640)
- Investment Experts (1,530)
- Research Experts (1,490)
- Technology Experts (1,470)
- Design Experts (1,320)
- Writing Experts (1,300)
- Travel Experts (1,210), etc.

I also discovered that not all Experts were equal in their level of expertise and their level of positioning in their respective market niches.

Some were very knowledgeable in many areas, but could not be called "Experts", as they were not really focused on any specific area of knowledge. Others were trying to specialize in one subject, but did not have enough practice, so they could only be called "Expert Trainees".

I decided to come up with my own definitions of the 3 major Market Segments that I have discovered, and I called them Aspirants, Positionists and Globalists.

"Aspirants" - Generalists and Specialists that aspire to become Experts
"Positionists" - Experts who want to position themselves in their target markets
"Globalists" - World Class Experts who care about the world we live in, who want to contribute and bring clients and global

experts communities together and who want to reach success and prosperity for themselves while doing it.

I also discovered a great number of various Global Experts Communities that all slightly differed in their value proposition, the type of services they provided and their agenda.

There are a lot of Expert communities out there, such as Experts-Exchange, BitWine, Liveperson, Expertist, Agora, TechRepublic, etc. All these communities are attempting to monetize the experts' knowledge, but do not offer a complete promotional machine that would help experts themselves become better experts, position them in their target markets or help them expand their client base globally.

The problem of all these communities is that they are either *Client-centric* (Experts-Exchange, BitWine, Liveperson), i.e. they are serving the client's needs—not experts' needs, or *agenda-based* (Expertist's agenda is helping experts **find projects faster,** Agora's agenda **is monetizing experts to sell their knowledge** in a newsletter format, TechRepublic's agenda is **promoting experts' articles** on innovation in technology, etc.)

None of the above Networks is Experts-centric, i.e. none of them has a strategic goal of providing leverage to the experts, none of them helps experts achieve prosperity through strategic market positioning.

There are Gurus out there that created promotional machines for themselves, but their systems are geared toward their core competencies and the Experts Community at large cannot benefit from those systems.

GLOBAL EXPERTS ASSOCIATION IDEA

In order to solve the Big Problem, I surveyed 100 Liveperson Experts and identified 3 biggest things that the Market was lacking:

1) Lack of Clients;
2) Lack of Promotional Methods;
3) Lack of Time to promote themselves

I've been thinking long and hard about the best way to address these "lacks" and I decided that the best way to solve this is to create a Global Experts Association focused on these 3 problems:

1) **Building the Network** connecting Clients to Experts and Experts to Clients, either:

a) directly (i.e. Clients post their Projects and The Experts are bidding on them) or
b) indirectly (i.e. the network's Advisors review Experts' and Clients' profiles and match them together)

The more Experts we introduce to the Clients, in order to give them a piece of advice, to put a solution together or provide help with their projects—the more they will give back to us in return.

That will solve "Lack of Clients" problem.

2) **Educate, Productize and Promote Experts' knowledge to the world** In order to educate Experts, explain to them how to productize their knowledge and how to promote their knowledge properly to their markets, I wrote *"The Secret Power of an Expert"*, The Expert Success Trilogy that lays the foundation for the continuity program and leads to creation of a Global Experts Association.

I also created a series of websites that invite Experts into one of the competitor's Networks, in order to educate them, build relationships with them and prepare them to the launch of The Expert Success Trilogy and Global Experts Association Network.

That will solve "Lack of Promotional Methods" problem.

3) __Build the Promotional System for the Experts__

In order to solve this problem, I started doing the following:

a) Identify major players in Business Process Outsourcing (Leverage and Scalability tools, Vendors, Strategic Consultants and Service Providers) and

b) Build Strategic Alliances and Joint Ventures with them.

Once the Global Experts Association Network goes live, these strategic partners will handle various parts of the Experts Promotional System.

That will solve "Lack of Time to promote themselves" problem.

THE UNFAIR ADVANTAGE

The Global Experts Association will give my Customers—Experts of this World—an UNFAIR ADVANTAGE over everyone else in their field.

Why do you need an UNFAIR ADVANTAGE?

__Being a "unique expert", well positioned in your Marketplace gives you an extraordinary power. And those experts that realize and achieve that power become extremely successful and prosperous people. And we know who they are.__

You also need to achieve that power, so that YOU would not have to work as hard as the others in your field, so that YOU will only focus on things that YOU LOVE TO DO anyway, so that YOU will have BETTER QUALITY OF LIFE than the others in your field, and so that YOU would be able to MULTIPLY YOUR WORTH even while everyone else around you in your business will fail and/or go bankrupt.

HOW WILL GEA NETWORK GIVE UNFAIR ADVANTAGE TO YOU, THE EXPERT?

#1. We will EDUCATE you, so that you could become a BETTER EXPERT

#2. We will help you PRODUCTIZE your knowledge, so that you could have a way of SHARING your knowledge with the world.

#3. We will help you collect 3 LEVELS of PROOF, so that you could PROVE to your target market that you a really an UNDENIABLE EXPERT that your industry needs that solves THE BIGGEST PROBLEM in your industry.

#4. We will help you create the LEGACY, i.e. an army of followers that will spread your knowledge in the industry like a wildfire.

#5. We will give you access to superior MARKETING, PR and MEDIA channels that will help you DELIVER your knowledge to the hungry market, by connecting you to the most successful and innovative promotional systems that can help you establish yourself as an Expert, establish yourself as an expert in your market niche and establish yourself as an expert in your field globally.

Chapter 22. Second Recap

Now, let's review the goals of Book One.

If you remember, my Goals were to prove 3 things to you in this book:

Number One Goal - to prove to you that Success is a Science—not an Art.

Hopefully, I was able to prove to you by now that your success has nothing to do with your talents, or your skills. It has a lot to do, however, with the realization that Success is a system.

Number Two Goal - to show you what you need to know for your success journey to be successful.

We went through the concepts of values and some Success Options for you to consider. I hope that by now I was able to convince you that, in order to achieve success that you desire, you need to create your own system.

Number Three Goal is to show you exactly what you should be focusing on in the start-up stage of achieving prosperity as an Expert.

Once again, I hope that, by defining and analyzing various business models, you were able to recognize the importance of building your own system, as opposed to helping others create their success—even if this realization might have been as painful for you as it was for me.

Yes—just like yourself, I've been dazed and confused before. Just like you, I did not know what I needed to do, in order to become and stay successful.

And if I shocked you with some of my revelations, if while reading this book you have experienced some serious "a-ha" moments—I can honestly say that I was able to achieve my goals and to show you a better way on your difficult journey to success.

What's coming in Book Two?

- In BOOK TWO of THE SECRET POWER OF AN EXPERT:

- you will learn why so many talented artists, musicians and scientists had to struggle so much in their lifetime, and why most of them died in poverty, while mediocrity laughed at them, reeking in cash and prosperity.

- In BOOK TWO of THE SECRET POWER OF AN EXPERT:

- you will find out what to focus on, in order to create massive popularity and gain a "super star" status literally overnight, while you are still alive—and not "post mortem" like many of your predecessors.

- In BOOK TWO of THE SECRET POWER OF AN EXPERT:

- you will learn that your resume is not what your clients want; they want to see the real YOU, your accomplishments and undeniable proof from other clients that YOU are the one they need to solve the big problems they have right now.

- In BOOK TWO of THE SECRET POWER OF AN EXPERT:

- you will learn that there is a way to create equal opportunities for both Companies and Individual Experts to promote themselves on a massive scale, and why this is now a reality—not a dream.

- In BOOK TWO of THE SECRET POWER OF AN EXPERT:

- you will learn that there is a number of marketing media out there that are eager to promote YOU—in YOUR marketing and sales efforts, and in YOUR market; you'll learn that there are plenty of companies like that, and their services are not that expensive—and that some of them would even do it for you for FREE!

- In BOOK TWO of THE SECRET POWER OF AN EXPERT:

- you will learn how to use Video Broadcasting as a uniquely superior method of self-promotion.

- In BOOK TWO of THE SECRET POWER OF AN EXPERT:

- you will learn why Direct Response is a uniquely superior and extremely powerful method of marketing, and why it works where everything else fails.

- even before you finish reading Book Two, you will be able to start promoting yourself immediately in a highly professional and desirable manner.

- In BOOK TWO of THE SECRET POWER OF AN EXPERT:

- you will learn that, by doing the right promotion, you can actually improve quality of content on Major Search Engines and Video Blogs.

- if, like myself, you are sick and tired of incompetence and lack of talent in modern society, you will have a chance to contribute to promoting professional approach in creation of video content on the Internet, TV and in other mass media channels.

- In BOOK TWO of THE SECRET POWER OF AN EXPERT:

- you will receive a unique opportunity to participate in creation of a new and trend setting self-promotion methodology and help position it in the minds of other experts, specialists and generalists.

- you will be offered an opportunity to help me educate society at large on the importance of being an expert in your field.

- In BOOK TWO of THE SECRET POWER OF AN EXPERT:

- you will learn more about the 6 Most successful and innovative systems I mentioned earlier in this book that can help you establish yourself as an Expert, establish yourself in your marketing niche and establish yourself as an expert in your field globally.

- you will have a rare opportunity to create industry standards in approaching video content and marketing on the Internet, all your friends and relatives will be jealous of you, whereas your clients will love you and want to stick with you forever!

Moreover, in BOOK TWO of THE SECRET POWER OF AN EXPERT I will be able to give you an Unfair Advantage over everyone else in your field.

Why do you need an UNFAIR ADVANTAGE?

So that YOU would not have to work as hard as the others in your field, so that YOU could only focus on things that YOU LOVE TO DO anyway, so that YOU could have BETTER QUALITY OF LIFE than the others in your field, and so that YOU would be able to MULTIPLY YOUR WORTH even while everyone else around you in your field would crumble and fail or go bankrupt.

Is that reason enough for you to pick up the Book Two? I will let you decide, my friend . . .

The Future Is Bright.
Keep smiling!

Yours truly,

Val Slastnikov

Works Cited

De Beers. (1947). Retrieved from Wikipedia, the free encyclopedia.

Albert Einstein Quotes. (n.d.). Retrieved 11 04, 2010, from ThinkExist.com.

Burnett, L. (n.d.). *Leadership Development*. Retrieved from Leader-Values.com.

Chances of Winning the Lottery - for Dummies ;-). (n.d.). Retrieved 11 06,2010, from Lottery Syndicate World.

Cobain, K. (Composer). (1991). Lithium. [Nirvana, Performer]

Covey, S. R. (1991). *The seven habits of highly effective people: Audio learning system application workbook*. Provo UT: Covey Leadership Center.

CSI. (2008). *Canadian Securities Course, Vol. 1*. CSI Global Education.

Daud, N. (2008, September 17). *Six Reasons Why Business Franchising Works*. Retrieved from KeepArticles.com.

Donald J. Trump, M. M. (2004). *Trump: Think Like a Billionaire: Everything You Need to Know About Success, Real Estate, and Life*. Random House.

Evoy, K. (2004). *Why People Fail*. Hudson Heights, Quebec: SiteSell Inc.

Farlex, T. F. (2010). *expert - definition of expert by the Free Online Dictionary, Thesaurus and Encyclopedia*. Retrieved from The Free Dictionary by Farlex.

Floyd, P. (Composer). (1973). *Time, The Dark Side Of The Moon*. [P. Floyd, Performer]

Franklin, B. (2010). *Benjamin Franklin Press*. Retrieved from Benjamin FranklinPress.com.

Gehl, D. (2008). *Prerequisites To Success!* Internet Marketing Center Inc.

Gemini, C. (2010). *World Wealth Report 2010*. Capgemini.

Headd, B. (2002). *Redefining Business Success: Distinguishing Between Closure and Failure*. Washington: U.S. Small Business Administration.

Johnson, R. (2007, 12 7). *Review Of Jeff Walker's Product Launch Formula*. Retrieved from Make Money From Home Online With Ray Johnson's Official Internet Marketing Blog.

Kiyosaki, R. (2008). *The New Rules Of Money*. The Rich Dad Company.

Kiyosaki, R. T. (2000). *Cashflow Quadrant: Rich Dad's Guide to Financial Freedom.* Business Plus.

Kiyosaki, R. T. (2005). Chapter 1: What Is the Difference Between an Employee and an Entrepreneur? In R. T. Kiyosaki, *Rich Dad's Before You Quit Your Job.* Business Plus.

Knopfler, M. (Composer). (1982). Private Investigations, *Love Over Gold.* [D. Straits, Performer]

Knox, T. (n.d.). *Questions of Credibility.* Retrieved from World News.

Kristolaitis, J. (2006, November 07). *Work World: The pros and cons of becoming your own boss.* Retrieved from The Medium Online: The Voice of the University of Toronto at Mississauga.

Lincoln, A. (n.d.). *Abraham Lincoln Quotes.* Retrieved from ThinkExist.com.

Osterwalder, A. (2006, 11). *Business Model Template.* Retrieved from SlideShare.net.

Resources, n. (2007). nPresence Resources - *Pros and Cons of Internet Marketing.* Retrieved from nPresence.net.

Rohn, J. (n.d.). *Jim Rohn quotes.* Retrieved from ThinkExist.com.

Schefren, R. (2006). *Internet Business Manifesto.* Strategic Profits.

Schefren, R. (2008). *The Entrepreneurial Emergency.* Strategic Profits.

Schefren, R. (n.d.). *Strategic Profits Vault.* Retrieved from The Profit Vault.

Simister, P. (2008, 01 28). Rich Schefren *Business Growth System Review.* Retrieved from Business Development Advice.

Starak, Y. (2006, 08 07). *Butterfly Marketing Manuscript Review.* Retrieved from Enterpreneurs-Journey.com.

Starak, Y. (2006, 10 19). *Your Last Chance To Get Into StomperNet Is Today.* Retrieved from Entrepreneurs-Journey.com.

Time Management Secrets: Getting More Done. (n.d.). Retrieved 11 02, 2010, from Paul Lemberg's Blog.

Tremayne, P. (2010). *Mass Control Revealed.* Retrieved from Peter Tremayne's The- Profit-Club.com.

Unknown. (2006). Retrieved from Yahoo!Answers.

Wikipedia. (2010, 11 02). *Affiliate Marketing.* Retrieved from Wikipedia, the free encyclopedia.

Wikipedia. (2010, 10 20). *Failure.* Retrieved from Wikipedia, the free encyclopedia.

Wikipedia. (2010, 10 10). *Self-employment*. Retrieved from Wikipedia, the free encyclopedia.

Wikipedia. (2010, 11 06). *Strategic Planning*. Retrieved from Wikipedia, the free encyclopedia.

Wikipedia. (2010, 11 02). *Success*. Retrieved from Wikipedia, the free encyclopedia.

Wikipedia. (2010, 11 01). *System*. Retrieved from Wikipedia, the free encyclopedia.

Wikipedia. (2010, 10 30). *Systems theory*. Retrieved from Wikipedia, the free encyclopedia.

Wikipedia. (2010, 09 07). *Value*. Retrieved from Wikipedia, the free encyclopedia.

Wikipedia. (n.d.). *Business model*. Retrieved 10 04, 2008, from Wikipedia, the free encyclopedia.